W. P. (William Paton) Mackay

Abundant Grace

W. P. (William Paton) Mackay

Abundant Grace

ISBN/EAN: 9783743313279

Manufactured in Europe, USA, Canada, Australia, Japa

Cover: Foto ©ninafisch / pixelio.de

Manufactured and distributed by brebook publishing software
(www.brebook.com)

W. P. (William Paton) Mackay

Abundant Grace

ABUNDANT GRACE.

ABUNDANT GRACE.

SELECTED ADDRESSES

BY

REV. W. P. MACKAY, M.A.

Author of "Grace and Truth, etc.

"HE BEING DEAD YET SPEAKETH." (Heb xi. 4.)

TORONTO, CANADA:

S. R. BRIGGS,

TORONTO WILLARD TRACT DEPOSITORY, COR. YONGE
AND TEMPERANCE STREETS.

1885.

Yours very truly
W. P. MacKay

PUBLISHER'S NOTE.

THE addresses which appear in this volume have been carefully selected from reports of Christian Conferences, held in Canada, United States, and Great Britain, with an occasional article from the religious press. Many of these addresses were personally revised by our departed brother, while on his visit to Canada.

This volume is now sent forth with earnest prayer, that He who is "the Way, the Truth, and the Life," may bless the truths therein contained.

The Publisher acknowledges his indebtedness to Rev. A. B. Mackay, of Montreal, for the photograph, from which the frontispiece has been engraved; also for newspaper, and other articles, from which material was secured for the biographical sketch.

PREFATORY NOTE.

BY REV. JAS. H. BROOKES, D.D.

THE following addresses will be found to possess a seven-fold charm for believers. They exhibit a rare knowledge of the Gospel, they are thoroughly scriptural, they are so simple a child can understand them, they are very instructive, they are fragrant with the name of Jesus, they are warm with the breath of the Holy Spirit, and they are most comforting. The pilgrim journey of the beloved and lamented author was soon over, but if the value and duration of mortal existence can be estimated by true testimony faithfully borne, by earnest work nobly done, he lived much longer than most men who have reached their three score years and ten; for in his powerful book, "Grace and Truth," and in these precious memorials, "He being dead, yet speaketh," and will continue to speak until Jesus comes.

All who heard him, must have been profoundly impressed by his intense zeal for the honor of Christ, and by his tender yearning for the souls of men. Nor was his anxiety confined to those who have never made a "profession of religion," as it is called, but his concern reached out to the vast multitude that gave no evidence of an experience beyond such a poor and paltry profession. Indeed the latter need to be pitied and prayed for, no less than the former. They are certainly in no less danger, nay, they are in greater danger, because their dread of judgment has been lulled to sleep by an empty "form of godliness," from which it is to be feared they will not awake, until startled by the thunder crash of the last day. Many, not few, but many in that day will plead that they have preached and done wonderful works in the name of Jesus, who will meet their plea with the words of doom, "I never knew you."

The most appalling sentence in the Bible is, "I know thy works, that thou hast a name that thou livest, and art dead."

The modern Elijah, some of whose utterances are here preserved, was bold as a lion in seeking to arouse slumbering "members of the church." He was altogether indifferent to human applause or censure; and it was obviously his aim to finish his course with joy, and the ministry which he had received of the Lord Jesus, to testify the gospel of the grace of God. Every sermon he preached, every page he wrote, glowed with the spirit of entire consecration that led the Apostle to exclaim, "To me to live is Christ, and to die is gain"; and the subject of his last discourse on earth, "The glory of God," towered before him like a pillar of cloud by day, and a pillar of fire by night.

Many will recall with sad interest now, the stirring appeals he made in Chicago during his last service in America. In one of them he said, "If ever I utter the words 'I think', when speaking to the people, I hope they will go to sleep, and remain asleep, until I have done with thinking. We are not to give men our thoughts, but God's words." At another time he was describing the splendid cathedral of Cologne, which he had recently visited with a friend. "What are those letters just beneath the top-most stone of that lofty tower?" asked Dr. Mackay. "I see nothing," replied his companion. "Then I will tell you what they are: 'RESERVED FOR FIRE,'" shouted the ardent preacher. These two statements explain the meaning of the book now offered to the public. It does not give man's thoughts, but God's words. It is also the final testimony of one on whose heart and lips, eternity was burned with a live coal from off the altar, shrivelling up everything earthly into utter insignificance. With him the hope of our Lord's return was a vivid reality; and though he was not permitted to remain until that promised advent, he is still waiting for it in sure and blessed expectation. In the light of this bright hope, growing brighter every moment, we may well say,

> " Oh! false, ungrateful words, to call the grave
>   Man's long, last home !
> 'Tis but a lodging held from week to week
>   Till Christ shall come."

St. Louis, Mo., U.S.A.

MEMORABILIA.

BY MISS ANNIE MACPHERSON.

M Y dear friend,—Your pressing letter requesting me to recall brief memories of our beloved brother the late Dr. Mackay of Hull, I cannot refuse, though in the very heat of departure for the thirty-fourth voyage across the deep waters.

I open my Bagster pocket Bible, and on the first blank page there is the following text, placed there by Dr. Mackay, when it was given to me in '75 by the pence of 200 of our poor east end widows. He said, "It was the verse he much loved, and that it was greatly needed by all Christians in these days of so much talking about the higher life, what we required was more of the lower life, lying down in the green pastures, feeding upon His own words, drawing our strength therefrom." "WITH ALL LOWLINESS AND MEEKNESS, WITH LONG SUFFERING, FORBEARING ONE ANOTHER IN LOVE." Eph. iv. 2.

Again, the last letter received is from a fellow-worker travelling in Scotland, and who was privileged to hear Dr. Mackay's last sermon. She writes, "We remained in Oban over another Sunday on purpose to hear him again, when on Saturday the sad news of his death arrived. He had preached to the Oban volunteers on the previous Sunday morning, and though pouring wet, as also in the evening, the place was crowded out on both occasions. His text was, in the morning, "Fight the good fight of faith," and in the evening it was, "Glory to God in the highest and on earth peace, goodwill toward men." On the first his points were these: 1. The Enrollment. 2. The Drill. 3. The Armour. 4. The Battle

In the evening he seemed as though he could not leave off, and then left his discourse to be *finished* the next Sunday evening. As it was, he gave us ten sermons in one, soaring into flights of eloquence, as he tried to tell us of the glory of God, and closing with such a simple Gospel as he said, "*I speak as a dying man to dying men.*" He then told how God could not be merciful at the expense of justice, and illustrating by Daniel going down to the den—how law had been kept &c., &c. I seem to hear his voice ringing out—"I through the law am dead to the law"—and now he said, the poor sinner had not to come and steal a pardon while justice slept, but mercy handed a pardon on the point of the sword of justice.

His theme ever was one of "mercy and judgment," holy apostolic boldness, which spared no pains or strength to win opportunities to proclaim the Gospel.

During the first six months of '75 he had travelled 6000 miles by rail, preaching the Gospel in the British Isles, returning very frequently in the middle of the night, to be back to his own church on the Sabbath.

All other themes and efforts he considered were not to be compared with the spread of the Gospel. On one occasion I was labouring in Hull for a week of services in connection with the Ladies' Gospel Temperance Work, and finding that Dr. Mackay's was the only church that had no Band of Hope gatherings for the young, I pleaded earnestly with our late dear brother, but he ever met all my arguments with, "That's not the Gospel, that is not the Gospel"—to the great regret of his fellow Christians, who longed for his influence. Once returning from the Believers' meetings in Dublin, accompanied by my brother-in-law Mr. Merry, we travelled from Holyhead to Chester, with Dr. and Mrs. Mackay, and for two hours we compared life-notes upon our first lessons in *trusting* our God for *temporal* as well as spiritual answers to prayer. In turn we told each other of the wondrous faithfulness of our God—making good that promise, "I WILL NOT FAIL THEE NOR FORSAKE THEE." Seldom do those who are but stewards of His silver and gold, know the trials of those who live many lives in one for the salvation of the souls of others.

When a student, and not long converted, Dr. Mackay's soul longed to tell others the story that had melted his own proud heart. He had heard of Duncan Mathieson the Evangelist, being at a fair preaching to crowds. He determined to go and join him, and offer his best—reaching the railway station he found that he had five shillings in his pocket, the exact amount required, leaving him not another fraction. But he had a simple trust that his Heavenly Father knew all about it, and all would be well. All day long he preached, and at eve an old weaver accosted him, and offered him hospitality, and half of a bed in an old garret in the name of the Lord. The next morning he was crying to the Lord to guide his way, and if he was worthy to preach the blessed Gospel would He open His gracious hand and supply his child's present wants. Bidding the kind weaver farewell, he went down the street where he was, when a young man who had heard him preach the previous day met him, and said the Lord has told me to give you that,—laying a golden sovereign in his hand, and thanking him heartily for the words of eternal life.

With his wants thus supplied, the young convert proceeded to the next place where Duncan Mathieson was holding outdoor services. The Lord had accepted his desire to spread the glorious news of salvation. All "lowliness and meekness" was the glowing charm of this bold and valiant servant of God. He had a fascination for the tender and reserved spirits whom he had probed out of their shells by using the sharp sword of the spirit with dexterous might. The "fearful and unbelieving" I have known would write and ask (to them) the most puzzling questions, and have their reply most speedily.

To our poor struggling east London widows, two hundred of them was not too small a crowd to draw forth the whole heart and strength, and for a whole evening, of our beloved brother. Although they were poor and old he suited his Gospel message and made them all so happy, and the hearts of the workers burned within them as he talked of his blessed Lord.

On one occasion asking Dr. Mackay if he could at all account for the great blessing that had accompanied his writing the book, "Grace and Truth." He replied, "I cannot explain it, only this I know, that I was ten long years writing it. When I found myself in the company of good and well instructed men, I would introduce the subject of one of its chapters for conversation: and any fresh light gained, home I went and re-wrote the chapter once more, accompanying this by much prayer and proving by the Word.

We mourn the mysterious providence that has removed this "instructed scribe" and able preacher and writer, from our midst, especially when the truth as it is in Jesus is being assailed upon all sides, iniquity abounding, and the love of many waxing cold. May the addresses now being published strengthen thousands to "arise and shine for their Light has come"— waiting, watching and working as those who may be ushered the next moment into the great eternity.

> "Be brave, and dare to stand alone
>   Against the foe,
> Thy Saviour stood alone for thee
>   Long long ago ;
> Be not a coward in the fight
>   Look up ! be strong !
> The morn of victory is near,
>   The Day of Song ! "

Boy's Home, Stratford, Ont.
    Sept. 30th, 1885.

BIOGRAPHICAL.

THE late Rev. Dr. Mackay was born at Montrose, and was educated for the medical profession, but his tastes led him rather in the direction of the ministry than the practice of medicine, and when about 30 years of age he gave up the latter for the former, though at the time he accepted the call to the Church at Hull, he was qualifying at Edinburgh for his M.D. diploma, the examination to obtain which he passed after he had gone to Hull, and was ordained a minister. His aptitude for evangelical mission work was first noticed by Prof. J. Y. Simpson, the inventor of chloroform, who encouraged him to exercise his powers in that direction. He subsequently, while passing through college, became associated with the celebrated Scotch evangelist, Duncan Mathieson, in whose mission through Scotland and Ireland he took an active part, working with much earnestness and success. He afterwards wrote his little book, "Grace and Truth," which obtained a very wide circulation, and created considerable stir in a certain section of the religious world. It had, we believe, a powerful effect upon the mind of Mr. D. L. Moody, evangelist, exercising an important influence in regard to many of his views, and giving him an impetus in the prosecution of the mission work he had already commenced. The circumstances attending Dr. Mackay's settlement in Hull were characteristic of the man. The founders of the Presbyterian Church at present worshiping in the elegant edifice in Prospect Street were at the time—now about sixteen years ago—occupying the Royal Institute. They were comparatively few in number, but earnest and vigorous ; and Dr. Mackay having paid them a visit for the purpose of occupying their pulpit for three Sundays, they were so impressed by his manner, that he was just the man to build up a new cause, they decided upon giving him " a call." This invitation was signed by twenty-four persons. Mr. Mackay had then determined to devote his life to the ministry, and was already so popular in the Presbyterian denomination that he had received similar calls from other churches, some signed by hundreds of persons; but he decided to accept that from Hull, because, he said, the congregation at that place was the weakest that had called him. Having been ordained a minister, he took up his abode in Hull, where he resided up to the time of his death, his pastorate of the church there being his first and only one. Shortly after he went to Hull the church at the corner of Baker Street and Prospect Street, erected by the congregation presided over by Rev. Andrew Jukes, was for sale, and being offered to the newly-established Presbyterian congregation, it was purchased by them. Upon the new building being occupied, Dr. Mackay quickly gathered around him a large congregation, amongst whom he laboured with much success. He was greatly beloved by his church, which comprised some of the most earnest and energetic Christian workers in the town.

Dr. Mackay was a man of strongly marked individuality of character, of a naturally buoyant and hopeful disposition, of great energy and capacity for work, and of great robustness and penetration of intellect. He had the gift of mastering any subject to which he devoted his attention, and had the wonderful faculty of making an abstruse and difficult subject clear and intelligible by the ordinary mind. Any persons who have read his book " Grace and Truth " will be able to form a pretty correct idea of his style of preaching.

For fourteen years he took no fixed income from his church. He took what friends chose to give towards ministerial support through means of a box placed in the lobby of his church. This arose largely from his unselfish, self-denying spirit, and from a desire that his congregation might be able to give more liberally to the extension of the Saviour's kingdom at home and abroad.

Not only amongst his own people was he popular, but there was not a congregation in Hull where he was not well known and always heartily welcomed, his face being perhaps more familiar on the public platforms of the town in connection with religious enterprises than that of any other minister in Hull. His services were sought for all over the country, and he was always a prominent figure in the Perth, Dublin, and Mildmay conferences. On two occasions he visited America for the purpose of attending similar conferences. On the occasion of Messrs. Moody and Sankey's first visit to Great Britain he took part in their mission both in London and Edinburgh, this being work in which he delighted, and in which he excelled, his labours in connection therewith being often carried on beyond what should be the ordinary limits of physical endurance, his capacity for work appearing almost inexhaustible. His style of exposition and address was unique, and his matter bristled with illustration and anecdote, drawn from his long and varied experience, and capacious memory. He was often abrupt, sometimes startling his hearers by the oddity of his expressions, and frequently humorous. His fervid rugged eloquence at all times compelled the attention of his audience, whether he was speaking from the platform or the pulpit; and his congregation never left without having learned some fresh truth or gained further insight into an old one. In private life he was exceedingly genial, and could converse with ease and accuracy on topics of all kinds, his fund of anecdote rendering him a pleasant companion.

Dr. Mackay was an earnest student of the Scriptures, and while he ever maintained that the Bible is its own best interpreter, he had no sympathy with those who claimed that they needed not the help afforded by the labors of others in connection with its study. He availed himself of every possible help, and all gained by him, he at once turned into current coin, and passed it into circulation among others.

Men eminent in Christian work—Mr. D. L. Moody with others—have acknowledged their obligations to Dr. Mackay as a teacher of the English Bible, and have preached the Word with greater fulness and certainty for having been closeted with him over the pages which present it to people's view.

His copy of the Scriptures became quite a curiosity. He called it "Enhakkore," after the water-yielding jawbone where-with Samson slew a thousand men. It was indeed the "well of him that cried." Bound at first in limp, he had it bound in boards, in view of work in the closet and in large meetings. The pages were blackened with constant thumbing, and ink lines under pregnant passages or across the page from one of these to another.

His constant study of Scripture in private was not the sole secret of his power as a teacher and preacher of Jesus Christ; but undoubtedly it accounts for a considerable portion of that power, and great success in doing good, which followed and attended its exercise.

It may not be generally known that to Dr. Mackay we are indebted for that soul stirring hymn :

> " We praise Thee, O God, for the Son of Thy love,
>   For Jesus who died, and is now gone above,"—

He was leading in prayer, at a public meeting. With a soul filled with gratitude to God, he, unconscious of any effort at poetical effect, made use of these words, and he was afterwards led to adopt them as the first verse of this now popular hymn.

Dr. Mackay was best known to the churches generally, as the author of that well-known book " Grace and Truth." It contains the substance of addresses given by him in the earlier years of his evangelistic labors. It has had an immense circulation in Europe, having been translated into many languages ; and English editions have been published both in Canada and the United States. Nearly a quarter of a million have been printed, all told.

But the faithful pastor—the loving husband and father—the earnest worker—has been called home.

The particulars of his death are as follows:—Having built himself a little villa at Oban, he spent his holiday there, if such his absence from home might be called, for he preached as often as the general run of ministers care to do when they are in full work, and he filled up the intervals between the services with divers employments. Tourists made their way to Oban for the Sunday " to hear Mackay preach," and the Free Church was always crowded when he was there, late comers being unable to find a seat even if they gained admission. From Oban, Dr. Mackay went for a trip to Thurso. The steamer called at Portree, and with some of the passengers he went on the pier. While returning, the night being dark and the lights defective, he missed his footing, and fell into the water, striking his head against the belting of the steamer. When he was rescued, he was quite unconscious, but in being taken to the hotel, he rallied. A beautiful trait of character was displayed in his request, made immediately after regaining consciousness, that his family should not be informed of the accident. The following night, congestion of the lungs set in, when a message to Mrs. Mackay was sent, and she arrived the next morning, only to learn that he was dead !

He seemed slightly to wander during his last moments, but his thoughts refused to leave the green pastures, and the quiet waters with which they were so familiar; and though these retreats may have seemed to his vision shrouded, as when the light grows dim, two precious landmarks were recognised and clung to. The first of these was " God is love," and the other " God is light." He repeated these over with great assurance shortly before his death, and made feeble efforts seemingly to gather other words around these. But he was now to deal with *realities* instead of with mere names. Instead of the mere vision of the light and love of God, by means of weak, earthly faith and hope, he was to feast his eyes on that light and love, as he stood where they see face to face.

One of the latest articles written by Dr. Mackay, for the British Evangelist,* (of which he was Editor,) was entitled " Change your money." In it he urged upon Christians to make a proper use of the talent of wealth, and he closed with these words:—" It is not an occasional or periodic earnestness that God desires, but a calm, constant, life-long work. A man moving about this world with the Holy Ghost within him, prepared for anything, at every step, by every look and word, testifying for his Lord, conscious of no effort, but living in calm peace with his Saviour God, in the unhindered power of an inner life, in the patient hope of a glory soon to dawn, is the type of God's true servant. His service does not depend on his rank, his circumstances, his position: these are all subservient to what the man is. He may be the wealthiest in the

---

* We have just received a letter from Mrs. Mackay informing us that this valuable paper, published monthly at one penny, will hereafter be edited by herself. She also adds that among the contents for the coming year will be Expositions of John's Gospel by the late Dr. Mackay. Leading thoughts on the International Lessons for the help of teachers. Gospel articles by the Rev. Dr. Fraser, London, and others. Persons sending address and one dollar to Mrs. Mackay, So. Morningside Drive, Edinburgh. will receive four copies monthly.

world, or have to sweep a street, but his joy in the service is the same. Such will have a natural entrance into the courts above, where the servants serve their Lord day and night."

"Dear fellow-servant, get so accustomed to serve your LORD JESUS CHRIST and Him alone, that your entrance into glory will not be unnatural, and thus an abundant entrance will be yours."

In no better words could we picture his own life. His was no "periodic earnestness, but a calm, constant, life-long work." He had become so accustomed to serve his Lord that his entrance into glory was not unnatural, but was an "abundant entrance into the everlasting Kingdom."

His funeral was the occasion of the expression of the loving esteem in which he was held, as well as of regret that he had passed away. Business was suspended, shops were closed, and the streets were lined with spectators as he was borne to his grave. From out the silence of the great grief which had fallen · upon the hearts of all, ears attent might still catch the lingering echoes of one of his latest utterances, as he lay a-dying—"For thine own glory !" In this language of confidence and hope there dwells a sacred solace for the friends he has left behind, which may well cheer them "till the day break, and the shadows flee away !"

CONTENTS.

THE GRACE OF GOD.

"For the grace of God that bringeth salvation hath appeared to all men, teaching us that denying ungodliness and worldly lusts, we should live soberly, righteously, and godly, in this present world looking for that blessed hope, and the glorious appearing of the great God and our Saviour Jesus Christ."—Titus ii. 11-13.

THE GRACE OF GOD.

THROUGHOUT these six millenniums of years God has been unfolding man's need of His grace. He has been unfolding His method of grace, and He is now unfolding His scheme of grace, and gathering the individual subjects of His grace, and will continue to do so until the great white throne is set, when sufficient specimens of His grace shall be gathered from the east, and from the west, and from the north, and from the south, to sit down with Him in the glory yonder, "that in the ages to come He might show the exceeding riches of His grace." I have oft-times thought that this is a precious idea connected with the Grace of God, that God has saved us not so much out of pity and compassion to us, but that He might manifest Himself and show forth His own glory.

In visiting the British Museum, those of you that have gone through it will remember how rich the collections are in the various departments of Natural History, Zoology, Palæontology, and all other departments where specimens are required to complete families, or orders, or species, or genera. What expense the British nation puts itself to in order to complete these species, or genera, in order to show completed specimens of all classes contained in a certain genus ; what money they will spend on what ordinary on-lookers think contemptible, such as little reptiles, which may be very worthless in themselves, but by their very collection they show the richness of the nation in gathering them together for the instruction of the people. If the British nation might send away to South America to get some interesting individual of some small insect to complete an order or family, look at what God is doing in these days :—He is gathering specimens of His grace from all quarters of the

world, so that in the ages to come there will be a number that
no man can number who will show forth the exceeding riches
of His grace towards us through Christ Jesus our Lord.   Poor
devil-chained sinner, will you not let God gather you in to be
a specimen of His grace?   He wants you, to place you in the
glory yonder to show what He can do, and how

> "His blood can make the foulest clean:
> His blood avails for thee."

He needs you, devil-bound sinner, for the great museum of **His**
grace, and I will tell you what—there will be no duplicates
there.   I have met some people who said, "Ah, there is nobody
that understands me; I am like nobody else."   I am glad to
hear it, because there are no duplicates in Heaven; there are
only special sinners up there, who needed a special Saviour,
and, therefore, are wanted in the big museum of Grace in the
glory yonder.

We read in Scripture of the prayers of two men: one of them
was the prayer of a Publican; the other, that of a Pharisee.
The Pharisee was thanking God—what for?   For what he was *not.*
The poor Publican could not even lift his eyes up to Heaven, but
he smote upon his breast crying, "God be merciful to me *a*
sinner."   No, that is very near it, but not what he said.   In our
translation there is a precious word left out and slightly altered,
"God be merciful to me *a* sinner" is not in the Bible, but it
reads, "God be merciful to me *the* sinner."   It should be the
definite article.   The man was definite: he tells God what he *is;*
while the Pharisee thanked God for what he was *not.*   And that
is the whole difference between a genuine prayer and a false one.
The Publican feels as though there was not another sinner in all
creation.   He gathers, as it were, in a focus the whole law of
God, and says, "I have broken it."   When we stand before God
as *the* sinner, we need a plentiful use of the definite article to
define ourselves right down before God.   It is this indefinite
business, this impersonal salvation that I have no patience with.

Firstly:—We have in this passage.   The salvation which
grace brings.   "The grace of God which bringeth salvation hath
appeared unto all men."

Secondly:—The lessons which grace teaches.   The grace of
God teaches us that we are to deny ungodliness and worldly
lusts, and that we are to *live*, not to *die.*

When I was a young boy, I thought that the good boys died and went to Heaven, and so I thought as I wanted to live, there was no use of my being good. It does not say the grace of God teaches us to die; it teaches us to live—soberly and righteously and godly in this present world.

Thirdly:—It not only brings salvation to us and teaches us lessons, but it also causes us to look for "that blessed hope and the appearing of the glory of the great God and our Saviour Jesus Christ." We have this salvation to begin with,—a life to live,—and a hope to look forward to; and all brought down to us by the grace of God. "Now the grace of God that bringeth salvation hath appeared unto all men," &c.

It would be utterly hopeless on my part to suppose that I shall be able to do justice to these three subjects: I would rather direct your attention to the connection between the first and the second, and to the truths connected therewith. Sometimes we are apt to transpose the 11th verse and the 12th verse, and sometimes we are tempted to separate them. We must take care neither to transpose, nor to separate them. We must not put the salvation that grace brings subsequently to the lessons that grace teaches: we must get the salvation that grace brings before we are entitled to learn the lessons that it teaches.

This is of great importance, that we must first be enrolled in the army of God before we can be taught the warfare of God. God will not teach His enemies,—they would fight against Him. We must become His children before we are taught the rules of His house. We must be the saved of the Lord before we can learn the lessons of the Lord. We must receive the salvation of grace before we are taught the lessons of grace. Do not transpose them ; if you do you dim the entire lustre of God's grace. You must keep the grace saving before the grace teaching. But you must not omit the 12th verse after you have read the 11th. You must not begin to talk about the salvation of grace without following it up with the lessons of grace: you must not merely say,

"My happy soul is free, for the Lord hath pardoned me."

That is not the whole of it, my friends, that is only the beginning of it.

There are soldiers, those who have just got the Queen's coin, they are enlisted, soldiers no doubt, and enrolled into the army of Queen Victoria, but you would never think of putting these raw recruits in the front of the battle where the veterans are face to face with death.   No, they must know first, all about the drill.   I know it myself from hard experience; I had to go at it day after day when I was a volunteer for our noble Queen.   It seemed very odd to us to go this way and that way at the command of another, but I assure you that all British victories have been gained by that splendid discipline.

I remember a friend of mine who was in attendance at one of the classes in the University; he was one of the very few that came out scatheless from the "Charge of the Light Brigade" at Balaclava; he was one of the six-hundred that "rode into the jaws of death, though they knew some one had blundered."   I asked him, "What did you think when the charge was sounded?" He replied, "I thought nothing about it : I knew we had to go, and there was the end of it."   That is what we want among the soldiers of Christ who have been enrolled under the banner of the great Captain ; they need to learn the drill, the discipline which will enable them to contend successfully against principalities and powers and spiritual wickedness in high places.

So you see the grace of God saves us in order that it may teach us; it does not save us that we may live as we list, and do just as we please ; but that we may, day by day, and hour by hour, become indoctrinated into the lessons of His grace, so that we may live *soberly* and *righteously* and *godly* in this present world. With these cautions let me now consider the first division of our subject.

"FOR THE GRACE OF GOD THAT BRINGETH SALVATION."   I love that word *"bringeth."*   You lady visitors sometimes find out the joy of this, don't you?   There is a poor consumptive patient lying down, unable to move about; you have been visiting that poor man day after day ; when you want that patient to have a little fruit, don't you think it much nicer to take it yourself than to send your servant with it?   In the one case it is *bringing*, and in the other it is *sending*.   I like the *bringing* better.   God did not *send* His salvation, He *brought* it.   He did not entrust it to the highest angel, nor to the highest of all the everlasting host who love to do His will.   The grace of God *brought* salvation.   It was God Himself who, in the strength of His own pity, passed seraphim, passed angels, passed cherubim, passed principalities and powers, passed all those stars of night from the height of His eternal throne down, DOWN, DOWN, to become one of us; down

to our sorrows, our circumstances and our sins, until last of all
He became our Substitute on the cross, crying out, "Eloi, Eloi,
Lama, Sabacthani : My God, My God, why hast Thou forsaken
Me." "He was wounded for our transgressions, bruised for
our iniquities," "made sin for us who knew no sin." Ah! it
was only when He was along side of us that He said, "Come to
Me." He did not stand up in Heaven and say, "Come up here."
It was when the Son of Man came to seek and to save that
which was lost, that He said, "Come unto Me." You remember
that poor Jew who was lying in the ditch, left there by the
thieves; you know the parties that passed by on the other side
—Priests and Levites—their work had been done already, they
passed on the other side, nothing more to get. But a certain
Samaritan as he journeyed (although there were no dealings
between the Jews and the Samaritans) came to where he was,—
came to where he was, what a beautiful expression! Ah! so it is
with God manifested in the flesh. He came to us dead—dead
in sins as we were. He became dead for sin, and the dead for
sin came along side of the dead in sin and brought salvation.
Remember our only plea is that we are lost, our only
plea is that we are ruined, but He is come to seek and to save
that which was lost. It is only when the sinner gives
up all efforts to save himself, and feels himself undone,
wretched and good for nothing, it is only then that God finds
him. God has to bring him down to be without strength.
"When we were yet without strength, in due time Christ died
for—" whom? "The *ungodly*." No man on earth dare have
invented that sentence. That one sentence is enough to prove
to me that the Bible is true. "For the *ungodly*." What angel
in Heaven dare have written such a word? What devil from
hell dare have coined such a word? What sinner on earth dare
have conceived such an idea? He died not for merely sinners or
transgressors, but for the *ungodly*,—for those who were against
God, who hated God, and, let me add, who would kill God if
they could. That is the height of man's lawlessness. And yet,
Christ died for the *ungodly*. Oh! chief of sinners dare you be
lost? *dare you be lost?* If so, these words will ring in your
ears throughout eternity, for you heard that He died for the
ungodly, and yet you would not have Him.

"The grace of God bringeth salvation." *Salvation;* oh the

precious sound! But it has no meaning, but as we have its counterpart *lost;* for "they that are whole need not a physician."

Look at Naaman, he had made up a beautiful programme of how he was to be healed; but imagine his disappointment when the prophet sent him word that he was to go and wash in the river Jordan. He thought that he would have come out and called upon the name of his God, and struck his hand over the place—perhaps, made some mesmeric passes, and that he would be healed. He had driven up with a magnificent retinue, and a splendid fee in his possession, and he thought he would have created quiet a sensation before this poor prophet. The great man's programme was knocked on the head: he must "go and wash."

Do you see that Naaman was not going as a patient, willing to accept the prescription that was given him; but he was going to prescribe for himself. The great beauty of our salvation is this, that faith uses what grace prescribes. The devil makes out sometimes that I am not a believer at all; he begins to argue with me and talk to me about my coldness, my indifference, etc. But I find there is a good way to stop all argument, viz., always to let my opponent have the talk to himself. I don't contradict him, and then he soon stops arguing. Ah, friends, there is no use arguing with the great enemy of souls: he is far more experienced than a poor sinner like myself: we have not any chance with him. Eve in the garden, Noah when he became drunken, David when he sinned, Peter when he denied his Lord —all found that arguing with the devil only resulted in failure. Best let him have his own way, and have done with him altogether. I am suspicious of him. When he tells me I am not a believer, I do not turn round and tell him I was converted at such an hour. When he shuts the believer's door, I run in at the sinner's door.

Mark you, friends, I do not depend upon my faith to save me; I do not depend upon the fact that I was converted to save me; I depend on the person of the Lord Jesus Christ to save me here and now; it is a present salvation. So when Satan would raise doubts in my heart that I am not a believer, and that I am a sinner, I tell him, "By your own showing I am a sinner, but by the infallible word of God I find that Christ died, not to save believers, but to save *sinners.*" Glory be to God in the highest! I come as a sinner every day to the blood which cleanseth, and

I cry "I the chief of sinners *was*"—no, no, the Apostle Paul uses the present tense, "*am*." "This is a faithful saying and worthy of all acceptation that Christ Jesus came into the world to save sinners, of whom I *am* chief." "I the chief of sinners am," so sang dear John Wesley, (they were among his last words) "but Jesus died for me." Ah, it is our loss that makes that salvation so precious; it is "nothing but Christ."

Many people are trying to work their way up out of the horrible pit that the Psalmist speaks about. We don't work *for* our salvation from the pit; it is on the rock that we work *out* our salvation. We are saved before we begin to work. In the days of Christ there were two classes of people spoken of, the Jews and the Greeks—the Jews requiring a sign and the Greeks seeking after wisdom. And these two have their representatives in modern times. There is Mr. Rationalist; he thinks that man is an intellectual being, and has to be educated and elevated. He says the three "R's" are indispensible, and then he begins to teach him the higher branches, to tell him about conic-sections, spherical trigonometry, Latin, Greek, German and French, until he becomes quite an educated sinner; but he is still down in the horrible pit and miry clay, and he is no further up than ever. Then again, there is Mr. Ritualism depending upon his ceremonies. He thinks that this being down in the pit is a devotional being, and that he must be devotionalized, and so he gets the dim religious light, the music, the millinery, machinery, and gymnastics, and things of that sort; and now the poor fellow begins to be devotional and to kneel as solemn sounds come across his ears. He is a devotional sinner, but still a sinner in the pit after all; and with all his devotionalism, unsaved.

Now, friends, our argument is this, that man is not merely an intellectual being to be educated, nor a devotional being to be devotionalized; but a *lost* sinner that must be saved or damned to all eternity. And here we find the grace of God coming in and bringing salvation to men, reaching down to him in that horrible pit the Gospel rope-ladder by which he can escape.

People waste their time in mud-measuring. One says, "My foot is only covered with the mud, but look at that fellow, he is ankle-deep in it;" the one who is ankle deep in mud says, "Look at that man he is up to his knees in mud;" while he, in his turn, says, "I am not so bad as that man, he is up to the neck in mud." It is of no use to talk like that, here is a rope-ladder to help you all up from the pit. "Oh," says one, "I am as good as my neighbour, and better than many." Very true, perhaps, but that is only the difference between being up to the knees in mud or up to the neck; if you are in the pit, you need a rope-ladder that you may get out and get your feet on a rock, "for there is no difference." One man with decent boots on, and only one foot a little muddy, says, "I do not believe there is 'no difference.' Do you mean to say I am no better than that fellow there up to his neck in mud?" No, my friend; and very likely the man up to his neck will get hold of the ladder first, for he is so shocked at the mud that he is glad to get out of it; while the respectable man spends his time in arguing about the depth of mud he is in. It is not mud-measuring but salvation we have to do with, for "there is no difference, for all have sinned and come short of the glory of God."

I remember once swimming with some friends in Scotland; I had not measured the current, and they had got across; and I found my strength was giving way. My two friends saw the condition which I was in, and at once sprang in from the bank to my rescue. When they reached me where I was—just in time, for my strength was exhausted—they each put a hand under me. I at once stopped all my efforts to save myself, and I was carried to shore in that position. I was saved *from under*. That is just where Christ saves from, beneath; He saves from *under*. You must let go the last rag, the last tatter, the last hope, and let yourselves be saved from *under;* "for *underneath* are the everlasting arms" of salvation.

But we have lessons after the salvation.

Very briefly let me say, that the lessons which grace teaches are similar in completeness to the salvation which grace brings. It teaches us to *deny ungodliness* to begin with, and *worldly lusts*. If a conqueror enters the enemy's country and has plenty of forces at his command with which to reduce it into subjection, and he is determined not to go back; in the first place he gives orders to burn the ships and blow up the bridges, so that there shall be no way back. And so when you come to Christ, Christian friend, I advise you to burn the ships and to blow up all the bridges and make no provision to go back again; you are done with ungodliness and worldly lusts.

Ah, my friends, Christianity is something that has to be lived

every day: it is not something that can be put on and off at
pleasure. Some people, you know, put on their religion when
Sunday comes, taking care on the Sunday night to fold it away
in their religious drawers. No, my friends, that is not the way;
Christianity is something that has to be lived all through the week.
The grace of God teaches us to *live*. What we need to do is to
live, and *fight*, and *work*, and *witness* for our blessed Master. The
grace of God teaches us the lessons for three kingdoms. We have
a kingdom that is *within* us; we have a kingdom that is *around*
us; and we have a kingdom that is *above* us. The kingdom that
is within us is represented by the word *"soberly;"* the kingdom
around us, that is our neighbors, is represented by the word
"righteously;" and the kingdom above, is represented by the
word *"godly."* So we are to live soberly, righteously and godly
in the present world.

Soberly. We are enjoined to govern our own hearts, our
own spirits. "Better is he who ruleth his spirit than he that
taketh a city;" and so the exhortation is to live soberly. I think
it is a great disgrace to our morality that this all comprehensive
word has come now to be limited to a mere phase in a man's life;
the word *sober* has got profaned down to the level of a mere
abstinence from the intoxicating cup. When you say that a man is
sober—it is rather suspicious to say it. My friends, we must not
pull down God's word to our own use of language. This word as
used in the Bible has the widest significance. There is a word
to us that are young men, we are exhorted to be *sober minded*.
We are, some of us, apt to be so self-sufficient, and think we are
up to a thing or two, and to think of ourselves more highly than
we ought to think. We might apply this word to young women
as well, and exhort them to be soberly dressed. I believe that
the grace of God comes down to a young man's mind, and to a
young woman's dress, or it is nothing. I believe in bringing
down these high matters to every day life; to your eating and
drinking, and dressing and clothing. I am not one of those who
believe in uniformity of dress for Christians; but if we were just
to take that one word *sober*, it would cover everything beautifully
—sober dress, sober living, sober minded.

I believe that God in the creation gave us a principle that we
still have, though in our ruins, and that was this:—He made what
was in the garden of Eden "good for food and pleasant to the
eyes;" for God gives us good food; and what is pleasant, yet still

sober. I do not believe in Christians making guys of themselves. This exhortation also applies to old men and old women.
To those who have made money, be sober with your gold, and
if this is practised the dollar bills will not come away, as they do
in many cases, as if they were stuck all over with glue. It is to
be remembered that we are only stewards of the manifold
blessings of God; we are also to make to ourselves friends of the
mammon of unrighteousness. Old and young, whoever and
whatever we may be, we must never forget that the grace of God
teaches us to live soberly, and that this word covers all the
kingdom that is within us.

Righteously. This word has reference to the kingdom that
is around us, when we go down to the shop, or mingle up with
the world. It is a grand old rule, "Do to another as you would
another should do to you." If you are a merchant, everybody
knows that you have to get your profit; you have to live; but do
it in a fair way, *righteously;* let the word, *righteous*, govern all
your dealings; it is not twenty-one shillings to the pound, or
nineteen shillings to the pound, but it is twenty shillings to the
pound straight down and square all over—that is righteousness.
We are to carry the principles of grace right down to the domain
of the world. But there is with some people a misconception as
to this. A Christian has no right to demand help from another
Christian, if he happens to be in a difficulty of any kind, on the
plea that Christians are enjoined to bear one another's burdens.
He must remember that the Scripture says that "Every man
shall bear his own burden," and this principle applies to the
domain of the world.

Godly. This has reference to the kingdom that is above. I
am to be God's witness, God's representative, to manifest God
in the world. My life is to be like the sun shining in its fulness;
I am to carry salvation to the dying, hope to the miserable, and
help to the needy. I am to be God's exponent of liberality in
the world. Christ said, "It is more blessed to give than to
receive;" but this was never intended to be applied to business.
You dare not go to your shop, and write over the door, "It is
more blessed to give than to receive." If you did, your stock
would soon be gone, your coffers empty, and all you would get
would be the blessing. These words refer to the voluntary
outgoings of love in the heart when renewed by God's grace,
and it would never do to traverse this principle across a domain

where such principles do not apply. I believe there is no more powerful lever in connection with our personal sanctification than the giving of material wealth to the cause of Christ.

I believe the lowest ideal of existence is that which neither gets nor gives—a diabolic existence. A higher, but still a very low ideal of existence is that which gets all and gives none—the existence of unsaved men. But higher in the scale of existence, is the man that gets all, and gives some, and is anxious to give more, and wants to give all—that represents the Christian here below, who gets all, is giving some, and is anxious to give all, as he will do by and by. And lastly, the highest ideal of existence is He who gives all and gets none—*God Himself*. Oh, my friends, let us strive to imitate God in the luxury of giving. He gives as the sun gives, as the rivers give. From Him shall flow rivers of living water. Look at our Church schemes — why the money that is spent on tobacco in twelve months would go far towards evangelizing the world. And I believe that if ladies were to send the money that they use upon superfluous dress, it would do the same thing. I believe that the money spent on superfluities would do far more than all the money of our missionary enterprises is doing. It is a standing disgrace upon us who profess to live godly. I want to reach your pocket; I want your pockets converted. I am not pleading for any special object—so that I can plead on the merits of the question all the better. Let us live like God in this present evil world. The only representative of God here is the Christian. Are we manifesting Him in our deeds and in our lives? A cup of cold water He will never forget. Look at the widow who put in her two mites. She is always spoken of as putting in her mite, but she had two mites which made a farthing. It was the widow's farthing, and not the widow's mite, that she put in. The Holy Spirit is never tautological. He might easily have said that the woman had a farthing; no—but it said "that she threw in two mites, which make a farthing." She might have kept one and given the other. But no; she gave the two—all that she had. I believe that the divided state of her purse showed the undivided state of her heart, for she gave all that she had. I will guarantee that that poor woman's gift has brought more real coin into the treasury, than all the gifts that any man ever put in; it was a heart giving out of its fulness. Brethren, let us rise up to the manifestation of this divine unselfishness. Selfishness is sin, and sin is selfishness; unselfishness is God-likeness. Let us strive to have more of the grace of God in our hearts "which bringeth salvation, teaching us to deny ungodliness and worldly lusts, and to live soberly, righteously and godly in this present world."

Lastly, we should be looking forward to our only certain future and our happy home, "looking for that blessed hope the appearing of the glory of the great God and our Saviour Jesus Christ, who gave Himself for us that He might redeem us from all iniquity and purify unto Himself a peculiar people, zealous of good works."

GRACE AND TRUTH.

"*The law was given by Moses: Grace and Truth came by Jesus Christ.*"—JOHN i. 17.

GRACE AND TRUTH.

"THE law was given by Moses; Grace and Truth came by Jesus Christ"—or rather, *were* by Jesus—the *came* is not in the original. Grace and Truth found embodiment in the Lord Jesus Christ. Do you want to see perfect Grace and perfect Truth in one? Then we find them in the person of the Lord Jesus, and in Him alone. The law was given to prove men. Grace and Truth are here up in contrast to the law. The law was given by Moses. It does not say it came by Moses. It was given as a test to try what man was. Now we find that Grace and Truth have descended to this earth, and have been fully manifested in the person of the Lord Jesus. If you don't see this distinction, you will get into constant confusion about the use and place of the law of God. The law of God was not given to save men; it was given to damn men; the law was not given to bless men, but to curse; the law was not given with God's thought that we would keep it; no, but "that every mouth might be stopped, and all the world may become guilty before God."

I remember one day when I was crossing from Dublin to England, between Kingston and Holyhead, in one of the steamers there, I was admiring the beautiful scenery as we were leaving Kingston Harbour, when a gentleman came up to me and entered into conversation. He said, " You are admiring the beauties of this Bay." I said, "Yes." I found he was an intelligent man, and we commenced to talk about Natural History. I had been that season busily engaged in pursuing my medical studies at the University of Edinburgh. I brought my friend on from one topic to another. I presumed that he was a minister of the Gospel, which I found afterwards to be the case.

We talked about birds and fishes, &c. We did not begin about
Theology all at once. Then we got on the subject of Natural
Laws, the Darwinian theory. I was telling him that I had been
studying this, that, and the other, and we got on the consistency of God in all kinds of law. He then said something
about the moral law. He said, "How is it that when God has
made all these physical laws, men will not believe His moral
laws?" I let him take the lead ; I wanted to see where we were.
He spoke about the obligation man was under to obey that moral
law. "Where do you find that ?" I asked. "In the Bible," he
said. "The Bible, what book is that ?" I said. He said, "It was
a book from God." This was just what I had wished to bring
him to—God's righteous demands in law. When thus he began
a talk about our moral obligations that men were under
to keep the law, and about God commanding obedience to its
requirements, I turned round to him and said, "Honor bright,
have you kept it all from beginning to end ?" He replied, "Indeed, I have not." " Very well, then," I said, "it is all up with
you, you are done for, if the Bible is true, for what was the
Apostle Paul's statement, 'When the commandment came sin
revived, and I died' ; it was all up with the Apostle then. It
is no use of you going on and asking God to help you to
keep it, you have broken it once ; if you were to keep it all now
to the end of time it would be of no use, as you have broken
it already." He then asked me, "Have you kept it ?" "Oh, not
I," I said, " I never professed to have kept it." He then wanted to know what I was going to do. " What you are going to
do ? you have done it already, that's enough ;" the junction between heaven and earth is broken ; you have broken the connection between you and God ; that's enough. If I were a stone
mason and wanted to build a house, the size of the stones
would be a matter of great importance and consequence to me ;
but suppose I was a scientific man, and not a stone mason :
suppose I had to show, not what stone had to do with building
a house, but the nature and quality of stone ; if I want to deter-
mine its specific gravity, I would not need to take a stone a
ton weight into the middle of the ocean ; I would take a small
pebble and drop it into a glass-full of water and show the
specific heaviness of stone. The smallest stone would demon-
strate the quality of stone equally with the largest mass of
a ton's weight. So with sin ; it is not the *quantity* of sin but

he *quality* of sin that God considers ; 'he that offends in one point is guilty of all,' there is the Divine statement, and it stands to reason." So I explained to my friend that it was of no use, as far as obtaining pardon was concerned, of us trying to keep the rest of the law, for we had broken at least part of it and we were therefore done for ; if we had broken it in only one point we were done for. While I was speaking I was looking quietly over the bulwarks. He was getting rather excited. He said, "What then, do you think should be done ?" "That is a different question," I replied, "I will tell you—it does not matter what you and I think ; the fact is that the law of God is a sword hanging over both you and me, suspended by a thread, and it will be upon us before we know where we are." He wanted to know what was to be done. I told him that the law of God comes as an executioner, and the sooner the offender is executed the better. It is said, "I through the law, am a dead man to the law." "Why," I said, "I was hung with Christ on the cross eighteen hundred years ago, that was the end of me, and the law came and did its worst." "What is all this about?" he asked. "It is this," I said, "the sooner you know that the better—that it is all up with you as to law-keeping, and if the sword falls into you personally as you are, you are damned to all eternity." I told him the law came demanding a life, and that life must be given either in the person of the offender or in the person of a substitute—and that our only salvation rested in accepting Christ as our Substitute—it was our privilege to accept what He has done and suffered for us on Calvary ; all that He has done in His grace and truth ; all that is true of Him is true of me ; it is on the Cross of Calvary where the demands of the law were satisfied. I was crucified with Christ and buried with Him. He was crucified for me and His death is mine—His burial is mine. What the law says to the rebel is, "Thou shalt die." It is no use saying, "I will repent and do better,"—"Thou must die, die in Christ, or to all eternity in your sins ; to die is your doom."

I left him for a while, and went with some friends of mine to the stern of the vessel. A few minutes after, he caught sight of me, and came and took hold of me by the arm. "Come here," he said, "I want you to speak to those friends about what you have been telling me—about dying." So I went and spoke to them, and said that I was just upon the A. B. C. of the subject, that God comes demanding my life, and I must give it up either in the person of Christ or in myself to all eternity. The man all at once said, "Glory be to God, I see the Gospel now as I never saw it before, I am a saved man." When we landed he was so happy that we could scarcely get him ashore; he was almost leaping and dancing; he was praising God that the law had done its work, that it had demanded his life, and he had given it in the person of his Substitute—Christ. He asked me if I could sing, and he kept me singing until I was perfectly hoarse. He kept saying, "I was dead through the law that I might live unto God, I have been crucified with Christ."

The law was given to test man, to show man that he could not keep it; but we find that Christ not only kept the law, but magnified the law. Let me here say, my dear friends, that I believe grace was before law; the law came in by the way, as it were, parenthetically; but the first idea of God was grace. I do not believe that grace and redemption were any afterthought with God, but that they were the thought upon which the whole creation was moulded; that they were in the long eternity of God, before man loved man, or before angel loved angel, but that it was only during these six millenniums that the wondrous plan has been worked out; grace was not known in heaven before. Angels knew the meaning of justice; they knew the meaning of righteousness—these words so full of awe, when those angels who kept not their first estate were cast out from heaven. Ah! they then knew what rebellion against the Eternal meant. Well might they weep when they saw our first parents drawn captive by Satan. Is this, they might have wondered, to be another holocaust; another manifestation of righteousness merely? No, God is to show what grace means.

I have often witnessed illuminations expressive of the loyalty of the people. At one of these, on the occasion of the marriage of the Prince of Wales, Sir Walter Scott's monument in Edinburgh was covered with gas jets from top to bottom, and all Edinburgh was bright as day. But what a day that will be, when in the ages to come, there will be an illumination from one end of heaven to the other, when God will show forth the exceeding riches of His *grace*. Angels will gaze with wonder at the scene. And who will be the little jets sparkling with the manifold grace of God? You and I, my dear friends, andmillions of redeemed sinners, the Manassehs, and the Bunyans, and the Luthers, and a great number that no man can number; they are to be all filled with the very light of God; illumined with His grace. Angels will wonder; seraphs will adore; cherubs will again rise up in adoration, and the hosts of heaven will strike their harps anew to the glory of the infinite God, and the top stone shall be brought forth with shoutings of *grace, grace* unto it. The great word seen in that heavenly illumination will be—GRACE.

It is *grace* that we have been learning something about these six millenniums. And in our evangelistic efforts, my dear friends, we are trying to gather little jets to show forth the riches of His grace. "But God who is rich in mercy." He is not spoken of as rich in *gold;* that is only used as pavement in heaven, it is of no use for anything else up there. You had better make good use of it *here;* as up *there* it will only be trampled underneath your feet. Send it on then, my friends, to the glory yonder, "Make to yourself friends of the mammon of unrighteousness, that when ye fail they may receive you into everlasting habitations."

People talk about the Eastern question, and the Afghanistan difficulties, and all the rest of it. Well, perhaps it is just as well that the world should look after those matters, but we too, must look after ours, and this is what we are looking to. What is the rise and downfall of great kingdoms to the grace and truth in Jesus Christ, who came as the great revealer of the deep, deep bosom secret of Almighty God? "Grace and truth came by Jesus Christ."

And here let me say just one word, with all respect to our scientific friends. I love science and profess to be a devoted scholar in the school of science, wherever science can teach me, I love to learn. I love to ponder on the blue depths of the heavens with the telescope, or to study the minutest creation of God with my microscope. I believe in studying all that my Father has made, with all the aid that science can give me. I profess to be a devoted and reverent scholar in the school of science. I believe in science, and I believe in scientific men. I am not one of those who say science is dangerous; no science is dangerous, except science falsely so called. For instance, I believe in geology, and love to study it. But the facts of geology are one thing, and the inferences of so called geologists are another thing altogether. The facts of geology I love as I love my Bible; because the one is my Father's building, and the other is my Father's writing. But do you think that I am going deliberately to accept the assumptions of men who perhaps between two editions of their book will be 500,000 years out in their calculations. No, thank you; I do not believe in such flickering will-o-the wisps, but in the Sun to guide me. I believe in the facts of geology, and the facts of geology are not very difficult to find out. They try to make you believe that their inferences are very perfect and very deep, when they are only *muddy*; they would have you think that it is very difficult to find out the facts of geology. Indeed, there are very few facts. Their argument in effect is that a cook takes a certain time in laying one layer of pastry after another, so God must have taken ages to build the different strata of the earth's crust. Scientists talk about the theory of development, and in some respects what they say seems very feasible, but while Darwin & Company are very good philosophers, they are very clumsy as creators. While they keep to their own department we will listen to them but let them not enter into the domain of *creating*. Five minutes with the Creator Himself will tell me better than all their books. I would rather go to Him, if you please, because it is more scientific to go to the Being who was the only one there, than to go to a lot of guessers who have come afterwards. Theorists indeed, when they attempt to philosophize about creation. In order to help the Creator they bring creation down to the dot of a small microscopic object, or protoplasm as it is called, the minim of creation. But it must be remembered that it is just as difficult to create this minim as it would be an elephant. We say to science, we believe in what you can teach us, but when we come to our dealings with our Creator, then we come into a domain that you know nothing of. I do not plead either for the reconciliation with revelation, nor do I defend their seeming opposition. I neither try to say that science and revelation coincide, nor shall I be careful whether I say that science fights against revelation. In the domain we are now studying the science of man can have no place whatever. I say to science, God gives a revelation that you can either accept or reject, but regarding which you cannot use the methods of science.

The foundation truth that I have to plead for in the manifestation of grace and truth is this, that *God became man;* that

race and truth thus came by Jesus Christ. Where did ever
cience hear of that? It is outside your court, sir; it is beyond
he range of your telescope; it is beyond your measuring line;
cannot listen to thee, oh, science, when thou dost leave thy
epartment. *God became man*—you have no measuring rod to
neasure that; you can only accept it or reject it as a revelation.

The second truth is like unto it, *that Christ is risen from the
'ead.* These are our two foundation truths.

1. That God was manifested as man.
2. That man was raised from the dead.

And these two truths are referred to in the tenth chapter of
Romans, where it says, "Say not in thine heart, who shall ascend
nto heaven, that is, to bring Christ down from above; or, who
hall descend into the deep, that is, to bring up Christ again
rom the dead." "That if thou shalt confess with thy mouth
he Lord Jesus, and shalt believe in thine heart that God hath
aised Him from the dead, thou shalt be saved."

These are the works that have to be done before any one
oul can be saved. Oh, science, whom I love in thine own
Iomain, dids't thou ever hear of the resurrection; of a man
aken from the cross and placed at the throne of God? Dids't
hou ever hear of a sin-burdened man sitting down at the right
1and of the Majesty in heaven? When we enter this temple,
Idieu,—stand aside as long as we are in this holy place. When,
igain, we meet in our Botany, in our Natural History, or where
ever thou canst measure and examine, we will be friends again.
But in the meantime we are in the domain of the incarnation
ind resurrection. The incarnation manifesting grace and truth
o us; the resurrection giving us the right to enter into, and the
itle to appropriate all that grace, and all that truth. It is a
revelation from the Most High, the deepest, the brightest, and
:he best that ever came down out of the silence above.

I have sat in my little observatory, on a starlight night,
watching with wonder and admiration some of the pheno-
mena of the heavens, as, for instance, the nebula of Orion with
its unnumbered worlds, which appear even through a large telescope like a film; and sitting there, when all is hushed and no
sound of man's voice, no sound of man's tread is heard, I have
sometimes felt the silence to be overwhelming. The poets
used to sing of the music of the spheres, but it was only a
poetical idea, for no sound or utterance comes down. I have

then gone to my knees and thanked my blessed God that He has broken the silence, and that "God, who at sundry times and in divers manners, spake unto us by the prophets, hath in these last days spoken unto us by His Son," the manifestation of the Father, "full of grace and truth."

The creation that is above me, I cannot fathom it. I feel like a little child tossed upon a boundless sea, the heights and depths are far above me. I have to exclaim, "How can man by searching find out God, and who can find out the Almighty to perfection?" If I look at His blessed law, I find that all the thunderbolts of His justice are against me; I have deserved them all; I have deserved His wrath—eternal punishment; I have deserved "weeping and wailing and gnashing of teeth;" for His own holy law is against me. But when I hear whispers of love and whispers of grace and truth—a truth that comes to reveal me as I am, and a grace to reveal Him as He is—I stand under the shadows of His love. I feel that I can do nothing but wonder and worship, and the more I wonder the more I worship, and the more I worship the more I wonder at the height, and the length, and the breadth, and the depth of the love of Christ that passeth all knowledge. When Adam had sold his God deliberately; when he had wandered from God and chosen Satan, God might have left him to himself, but, no! God says, if you can do without me, I cannot do without you —Adam, where art thou? What a loving heart is shown in those words: I want you; I do not want you to go to Satan. There was an exhibition of grace and truth, before even the first gospel was preached. The activities of this God of love were the activities of grace and truth. And does it not remind you of the New Testament statements, that the Son of Man is come to seek and to save—what He seeks—that which was lost; and so He tells Adam what he is and what God is. Adam was afraid and went and hid himself, and the grace of God followed him, until the seeking God found the fleeing sinnner. I do not wish to prescribe for other brethren in the way of dealing with anxious souls, but you will pardon me if I give my own experience with anxious souls. For many years now, I have never told an anxious soul to seek the Lord. Don't go away with the wrong impression; I will explain it to you just now. It is certainly the bounden duty of every man, anxious or not, to seek the Lord, just as it is the bounden duty of every man to keep the law of God; but still while we find the Old Testament telling us to "seek the Lord while He may be found," what do we find the result as detailed in the third chapter of Romans? "There is none that seeketh after God." In fact the whole germ of the law is contained in the expression, "Seek the Lord," and the whole result of the law is found in the third chapter of Romans, "There is none that seeketh after God." But when we turn to the Gospel and study its Grace and Truth, the position is reversed. We read, "The Son of Man is come to seek and to save that which is lost;" which shows that it is the Lord who is the great seeker now, and who has come down in the strength of His own pity, and the activities of His own love. "And the Son of Man is come to seek and to save," and I will guarantee that He will find all that He seeks. But the moral responsibility rests upon you and me what to do, viz., to take the lost sinner's place, for it is only the lost sinner that lies in the pathway of the seeking Saviour, and thus can be saved. That is what I have to do; I have to accept the Grace and the Truth that came by Jesus Christ. The truth that puts me down guilty, condemned, lost, ruined, without a plea, without an excuse, without a palliation. He will do the rest. He saves for He is seeking to save. The Son of Man is come—the fulness of the Father, "full of GRACE AND TRUTH."

WHAT MUST I DO?

WHAT SHALL I DO FIRST?

" *What must I do to be saved.*"—ACTS xvi. 30.

———

" *Seek ye first the kingdom of God, and His righteousness ; and all these things shall be added unto you.*"—MATT. vi. 33.

WHAT MUST I DO?
WHAT SHALL I DO FIRST?

HOW often in your own history have you asked this question? Did you ever meet a man who has not asked it? If you could get into the inner secrets of all you meet in the street, you would find that the great majority are asking this question—What must I do? High and low, grave and gay, lazy and idle, good and bad, ask this question—*What must I do?*

The boy at school, anxious to get to the top of his class and obtain the prize, often asks it ; and when he leaves school to push his way, this is his great question.

The ship captain in the lashing storm, with the waves threatening to engulph him, and his canvas flying in tatters, has this question often before his mind.

The doctor, baffled by the disease in his patient, puts his hand on the pulse, gathers up all possible information, and having completed his diagnosis, resolutely says—*What must I do?*

The lawyer, anxious to bring his client successfully through, is often pondering the best arguments, obtaining fresh facts and witnesses, in answer to this question.

The merchant has his bills to meet, and you see him going hither and thither with hurried step the day before, and the question he asks of his confidant is—*What must I do?*

The engineer has been commissioned to lay a telegraph wire through the ocean, to send a canal through the desert, to bore a tunnel through the mountain, and, day by day, night after night he asks himself the question—*What must I do?*

The beggar, not knowing where to get his next meal ; the

queen on the throne ; the poorest peasant ; the prime minister, all in their spheres, are, day after day, asking the same question.

Shall we look to the drunkard, after he has pawned the clothes off his wife and children, ruined his body and damned his soul, without a copper, and turned out by the drink-seller ? He is revolving this question— *What must I do?*

So with the licentious man, the greedy man, the covetous man, with his lust or his gain— *What must I do* to have more ?

Look at that young lady, cursed with what many people think the highest point of blessing—"plenty of money and nothing to do." She dresses, goes to parties, undresses, dresses, and so on. As she stands miserable at the looking-glass, there is one question in her mind, and perhaps only one, and it is— *What must I do?*

In the village of Gravelotte, I sat in a peasant's house, in a chair in the corner of a window. The peasant's wife informed me that in that same chair and place, the Emperor Napoleon sat the day after he left Metz, on his way to Chalons, after he had heard that the German forces were rather nearer than he expected. For a whole afternoon he sat there and spoke not a word, but smoked his cigars and drank the black coffee which the peasant's wife could give him, and I know the question that was uppermost in his mind, and that was— *What must I do?*

Opposite this, in another small house, I entered the apartment in which King William, Bismarck, Von Moltke, and others sat, some days after, and planned that awful day's work at the quarries of Gravelotte, and the question in the King's mind was — *What must I do?*

Vanquished and victor, emperor and beggar, ruler and serf —all mankind—ask the question. Is it not a question peculiar to man ? Does it not hint that he is dissatisfied with present attainment, and is pushing onward to something in the future. No animal improves by failure except man. The swallow's nest in Noah's ark was just as good as the one in the eaves of your house. Man's longing after something better in the future finds expression in this question— *What must I do?*

We are most taken up with what most concerns ourselves. It is not what must my friends do, my brothers do, my neighbors do ? but, what must *I* do ?

This question increases in intensity in direct proportion to the amount of work to be done, and to the anxiety of the doers that it should be rightly done. Let us now look specifically at the greatest of all works, and ask. What ought I to do in order that I, a sinner, may get to heaven?

Sin has to be put away. What a statement! And we are sinners who love sin, and cannot, by nature, help loving it, and we have to do with a Holy God.

Sins have to be pardoned, and we have committed them. We are the offending and not the offended party, and we have to do with a righteous God.

Peace has to be made, and we have no power nor place in the making of it. We have to do with an all-powerful, all-truthful God.

A way has to be made into God's presence, righteously hid from sinful man by the sword of His justice, by the veil that shrouds His glory.

God's majesty has to be manifested, God's righteousness has to be vindicated, God's holiness conserved, God's truth maintained, God's law magnified, and we are unrighteous, unholy, untruthful transgressors.

Not only has every barrier to be broken down, a way made, and a robe prepared, but an entirely new nature has to be provided for the sinner—a nature that loves what the sinner used to hate, and hates what the sinner used to love; a nature native to heaven—"ye *must* be born again."

Self has to be set aside, denied, and mortified—and we by nature know nothing but self.

The world has to be overcome; and we were born in it, are part of it, and love it and its ways.

Satan has to be vanquished, and we are his servants, willing slaves, powerless beneath his allurements, weak against his wiles.

How can we, in sight of such work, ask the question, *What must I do?* God's authority all the while is demanding that all this has to be done; and if the callous conscience for a time forgets it, the demand is none the less imperative, the duty is none the less binding. All this has to be done; and I am a sinner who does not love God; an enemy, who cannot suggest the terms of peace; guilty, and therefore deserving wrath, and condemned already; lost, and unable to find my way; without strength, and incapable of righting myself; *dead*—the climax of all—spiritually dead in trespasses and sins. Let us now ask

—what could I do? Could I not pray? Then the prayers of
the wicked are an abomination to God. Could I not try to do
better, or repent? What does this mean from a dead man's
lips?

But I am doing the best I can; the works of righteousness
I try to perform in my own feeble, failing, faltering way. But
God says "all our righteousnesses are as filthy rags;" and this
does not mean bad deeds, but our good ones. All the righteous things I ever did, when looked at in the light of the work
to be done, are filthy rags. Can I not hope? If you are unsaved, you are without God; and if without God, you are
without hope in this world. You may think you have hope,
but it is a poor will-o'-the-wisp spectre and death-sparkle, allur-
ing you to the lake of fire—not the pole-star of God, set for the
guidance of His own tempest-tossed children.

Let us now look at the glorious good news. Carefully look
over all that has to be done; leave out no jot of it, for God
says it must be done, and there is no getting past it. Look
over our utter inability to do anything. Take, for example,
but one of the *must-be's*. "Ye must be born again." Confess
your entire helplessness, and then you are ready to hear God's
own glorious news concerning this work (John xix. 30)—"it is
finished."

Yes, God began it, and God ended it, and you and I have
nothing to do but to accept it, enter into the enjoyment of the
fruits of what He has procured. Look at these wonderful
words—

God says, "Ye *must* be born again."

The sinner says, "What *must* I do to be saved?"

God says, "The Son of Man *must* be lifted up, that whoso
ever believeth in Him should not perish, but have eternal life."

If we are to sum up shortly the immeasurable work to be
done, we find that there are two pillars on which the whole rests.

Our sins are to be pardoned; our sin has to be put away.
This, as it were, settles all that stands against us.

A new nature has to be given us, as our first nature is utterly
unfit to enter heaven.

God laid our sins on Jesus (see Isa. liii. 6). He bore our
sins in His own body on the tree. He was delivered for our
offences. He gave Himself for our sins. God made Him to be
sin for us. Does all this not satisfy you?

He has been raised again. We are invited to Him. We are made partakers of the divine nature. We receive a new creation by the power of the Holy Ghost. Is this not sufficient? Praise the Lord, it is.

God laid the whole case on Christ.

Christ bore it all, and settled every question.

The Holy Ghost now proclaims it to every creature, and urges all to accept it. Will you cease from your thoughts of, "What must I do"? and ask, What has God done? Must I not believe? Yes; and with many this seems to be the hardest of all works—a sort of toll that God demands to test our sincerity!

A friend one day asked me to take a drive and spend the day with him. I accepted his invitation. He paid for everything. As we neared the town, we had to pay a toll. Another friend sitting beside me, thinking I was to pay the toll, said—

"Mr.—— will pay."

"I should think so," I replied. "After having paid for everything, I didn't think I would insult him by paying the 4½d. of toll."

God has done all the work; but the striving, anxious inquirer thinks if he could only get up a tender heart, or a good feeling, or a little faith, that he would then be doing his part—paying the toll and accepting the drive. But God is the noblest of all givers. Let us be the simplest of all acceptors. Accept it for nothing. Do not come as a believer—one with good feelings —but come as a sinner, and listen to one of God's answers to "What must I do to be saved?" as found in Romans iv. 5 :— "To him that *worketh not*, but believeth on Him that justifieth the ungodly, his faith is counted for righteousness."

WHAT SHALL I DO FIRST?

We find in the Word of God that human nature is not subject to the will of God. The history of the world shows us a strange thing existing in it—a something that we cannot understand. That there should exist in this universe of God something called sin, and beings called sinners, is inexplicable to man, and has not been explained by God; the fact, however, stands, that we are sinners. The Apostle Paul calls himself "the chief of sinners." And we shall have to add "sinner" as part of our name ; but, blessed be God, we can add too, "saved by grace." The child of God starts with this as his first principle, that there are no contradictions in the Bible. We clear God at the expense of our own understanding. Listen to what God says in these verses, "Take no thought for the morrow ; for the morrow will take thought for the things of itself." Is this not a capital text for a lazy man, who sits down and thinks God will send him loaves of bread showered out of heaven ? This is to turn the truth of God to licentiousness. "Be careful for nothing." "Ah, well," says one, "I'll be careless of everything." Very well, friend, go on and do as you like. Write it on your table, and enjoy it for your dinner if you please. Faith sees another text, "If any would not work, neither should he eat." It is infidelity and man's evil heart that makes God's Bible read wrong. "Seek ye first the kingdom of God." And here we get a double meaning of this word "first." We must seek it *first* as relating to time, and seek it first as the most excellent at morn, noon, and night ; we have to seek the kingdom of God, and thus God gets his claim first met. What are you living for ? For God. Does that not ennoble the meanest toil ? "Seek ye first the kingdom of God."

I. What is this kingdom of God ? It is very little spoken about in Matthew. It certainly is mentioned several times, but it is not characteristic of the gospel. The great thing Matthew speaks of, is the "kingdom of heaven." In Luke we find it is always the "kingdom of God." When we speak of the "kingdom of God," one thing is meant, and by the "kingdom of heaven" another. As we usually speak, we see no difference ; but God does not write for the poetry of the sentence, but for the truth. When we talk of the kingdom of heaven, we mean the rule of the heavens, and thus get an idea of earth as contrasted with heaven, as we find it in the whole of the 13th of Matthew ; but the "kingdom of God" links in the whole character of God, not contracted by heaven and earth, or the Jew and Gentile dispensations, but it is the bowing of the creature to the Creator.

It is defined in Scripture (Romans xiv. 19) to be "not meat and drink, but righteousness and peace, and joy in the Holy Ghost." Therefore, "Seek ye first the kingdom of God, and His righteousness." This kingdom you see is *not* meat and drink. What, then, do you live for ? What is the meaning of your existence? Are you laboring with those hands, toiling in the sweat of your brow? What is to be the Saturday night of your existence? Are you merely to work to get money; get money for food and eat that you may get muscle to work again? What an animal existence! Nay, dear working man, God would have you take a far higher aim than food and drink, higher even than the princes of the earth. The kingdom of God is *not* meat and drink, therefore the poorest man may have the noblest aim. Seek it first; seek it everywhere—in business, in trade, in repose, in prosperity, in adversity. What a high position you thus have! No man can work like a Christian, for it is not for meat and drink he works, but for "righteousness, and peace, and joy in the Holy Ghost"—that is his aim.

The first thing that has to be settled since sin came into our world is the question of RIGHTEOUSNESS.

How can God be *just* and yet pardon the sinner? You can easily see how He can be merciful; but how can He be *just?* Many people trust to the *mercy* of God; don't lie down on that; there is no mercy at God's judgment-seat. What is to be done then? Look at those bleeding hands on Calvary—those bleeding feet and brow, and at that pierced side. Look at the debt paid there! Who hangs there? The spotless, sinless Son of God, manifest in the flesh. Ask the meaning of that sun clad in darkness, of the rocks riven, and of the veil rent by God's own hands right from the top to the bottom. What is the meaning of that awful agonizing cry, "My God, my God, why hast Thou forsaken me?" It means that, "*we* might be made the righteousness of God in Him." Ah! we have got the keynote now—not merely mercy and pardon, but *righteousness*. We are asked to seek "His righteousness"—God's righteousness is *first* to be established. That burden upon the Son of God tells me the debt is paid, therefore God can in perfect justice save the greatest sinner.

God is righteous in doing it, that "He might be just and the justifier of him who believeth in Jesus." Righteousness is one of the brightest jewels in the diadem of glory—that gem of untarnished justice—and the Christ of God "is made unto us wisdom, *righteousness*, sanctification, and redemption." Thus shall every saved soul show the exceeding riches of His grace, and the perfection of His righteousness.

The second part we consider, connected with the kingdom of God is—PEACE.

Peace with God, the peace of God, a peace made, a peace manifested in a person, a peace proclaimed as already made—

> A mind at "perfect peace" with God,
> Oh! what a word is this!
> A sinner reconciled through blood—
> This, *this* indeed is peace!

We have peace with God through our Lord Jesus Christ—not within our own breasts. We have no peace with what is not subject to the law of God. Peace with a heart at enmity to God—never! Did you ever feel the conflict that goes on in a man's heart? Before we had the righteousness of God in Christ, the fight was not with ourselves, but *with God*.

Now, too, we have the peace of God fortifying our souls. Many persons, looking at the heathen all around, and at the evil on every side that seems to be getting so bad, say, "they don't know what is to be done." But "when these things begin to come to pass, then look up, and lift up your heads, for your redemption draweth nigh." It is consistent with the hope of the Christian that "wicked men and seducers are waxing worse and worse." Seek that peace that God alone can give.

Lastly, there is Joy in the Holy Ghost. Jesus does not want us to go hanging our heads like bulrushes. A Christian ought to be the happiest man in the world. God says, "Rejoice in the Lord always;" but this is not the joy of false fire, of the theatre, of the concert, or the ball-room; the flesh never heard of the "joy in the Holy Ghost." You wish to be merry! Well, "if any one is merry, let him sing psalms." It is the joy that is found in the kingdom of God founded on righteousness, and manifested to the glory of God. Thus the pillars of the throne of the kingdom are acknowledged. Righteousness is the foundation, Peace is the state, and Joy in the Holy Ghost is the manifestation of the state of the subject.

II. We are told to *seek* it. Jesus the King has come to seek subjects. Where can I find the kingdom? Not within us, not around us, not at the throne above us, but in the person of Jesus, who could truly say of Himself, when on earth, that the kingdom was among them. In Him righteousness and peace have met, and seeking the kingdom amounts to looking to Christ. And since the incarnate Word has gone, I must find

Him and it is in the written Word, thus believing the record that God gave of His Son.

III. All things will be added. Men have turned this round. Seek the things of earth and eternity on a death-bed. The father tells his son—religion is very good, but see and get on in the world first, and sometimes not at all scrupulous as to the first elements of the kingdom, even righteousness. The *last* thing men generally seek is the kingdom of God. "Let all things be done decently and in order," and take God's order. Therefore, till a man has got the kingdom of God, he is in disorder. All his life is out of order. Earth, time, money, fame, honor, fill up man's thoughts, and hence the disappointment, misery, and eternal ruin. Deliberately, wilfully, they put last what God has put first. To the one who has entered the kingdom God promises all things. By and by, the saints shall reign over the earth; and, meantime, all things are ours, for we are Christ's, and Christ is God's. Meantime, having such title-deeds in our hands, we can well afford to wait and accept food and raiment with contentment, while we manifest the life of God in a world that rejects Him. In the discharge of our duty, in the labor to God, in obeying the principles and commandments of the kingdom, no good thing will He withhold from us. Reader, have you sought this kingdom *first*? If not, your whole life is a mistake. Seek it now.

JOB'S QUESTION, AND PAUL'S ANSWER.

"How should man be just with God?"—JOB ix. 2.

JOB'S QUESTION, AND PAUL'S ANSWER.

J OB, in his distress, raised this question, "*How should (can* R.V.) *man be just with God?*" (Job ix. 2.) The divinely-appointed sacrifices in Israel, the ancient idolatries and sacrifices of Greece and Rome, the modern abominations to false gods in heathenism, all tell out that conscience, as well as law, ever keeps before fallen man this fundamental question. Man has never, even to his own satisfaction, answered this question; so that, where he is conscientious, his whole life is taken up in seeking for an answer in his own efforts, and never finding one.

Paul has answered it, or rather God the Holy Ghost, by the pen of Paul in the letter to the Romans (iii. 26), where he tells us that Christ came, and shows how God Himself can be "just and the justifier of him which believeth in Jesus." Under several aspects do we find justification in the Scripture :—

> Justification by God.
> Justification by grace.
> Justification by blood.
> Justification by resurrection.
> Justification of life.
> Justification by faith.
> Justification by works.

1st. JUSTIFICATION BY GOD.—What a wondrous truth ! God steps in Himself and justifies the sinner. The process by which this is accomplished, and the vindication and manifestation of all His attributes in this justification, we shall shortly consider; but *the fact* is the first thing to take hold of, that God hath come in for our justification. "Even as David also describeth the blessedness of the man, unto whom *God* imputeth righteousness without works" (Rom. iv. 6). So also " *The Lord* hath laid on Him the iniquity of us all." (Isaiah liii. 6.) *God* is "the justifier of him which believeth in Jesus" (Rom. iii. 26). "Who shall lay anything to the charge of God's elect?" (Rom. viii. 33). Shall *God* that justifieth? And He only has the right to lay to our charge—but He justifies us. He is spoken of as "*Him* that justifieth the ungodly" (Rom. iv. 5). Man is going about trying to secure his justification. He will not stand still, and let God justify him. Jesus told the religious people of His day—"Ye are they which justify yourselves." (Luke xvi. 15). And as long as we are attempting to justify ourselves, we cannot submit to let God justify us. We excuse, palliate, cover over our sin, until we understand this fact, that it is *God* that justifies.

2nd. JUSTIFICATION BY GRACE.—God could point to unfallen angels, and say against all accusers, " These stand in creature righteousness," but He could not justify them by grace, for they never required it. In order to see the meaning of this expression, we must understand what and where man is, when God steps in to justify him. In the Epistle to the Romans, it is not until *all men in the world*—good, bad, and indifferent— have been brought in guilty before God, that God opens up His secret. It is not until man at his extremity cries, "How then shall man be just with God?" in the sight of His inflexible justice, and stern, unbending judgment—that God steps in and answers his question by opening up the treasures of His grace. The criminal has been found guilty at the bar, the judge has pronounced the sentence, the convict now awaits execution ; his prayers, his tears cannot save him ; he is condemned. It is in vain that he loudly calls for mercy, and promises amendment for the future ; the sentence has been passed—the law is inflexible, and his blood is demanded. Now it is the time for grace. The judge who has condemned, has planned the way by which the condemned criminal may become a loyal subject. He wishes to "show the exceeding riches of His grace" in His kindness to that condemned man. The thought arises in the Judge's heart : for it is for His own name's sake that He does it ; and thus we are "justified freely by His *grace*" (Rom. iii 24 ; Titus iii. 7). But what of the justice of the judge? Is it to be sacrificed ? What of the inflexible character of His law? Is it to be tampered with? Nay, verily. This leads us to consider—

3rd. JUSTIFICATION BY BLOOD,—He spared not His Son, but gave Him up to death 'or us,(blood being the emblem for "life taken"). So we are spoken of as "being now justified by His *blood.*" (Rom. v. 9). Death has been demanded. Christ has died; the penalty has been paid. So, if "we are justified freely by His grace," it is "through the redemption that is in Christ Jesus; whom God hath set forth a propitiation through faith in His *blood.*" (Rom. iii. 24, 25). Man could tolerate a certain kind of grace, or an interest in Christ's holy life, but he cannot bear the "blood" theology. But the key-note of God's justification is blood. Blood is the procuring cause, as this passage proves to a demonstration. The judge was gracious; therefore He gave His Son for the criminal. The Judge was just; therefore He could not spare the life of His Son. God's justice is now displayed to the universe in the blood of His Son, as nowhere else it could be seen. It is according to the positive value of this precious blood that we are now justified. God's justice demanded death; God's grace provided blood. So the obedient One, under all the load, says, "But thou art holy, O thou that inhabitest the praises of Israel!" (Ps. xxii 3.) He vindicates God while He feels the judgment stroke pouring out His precious blood, and thus puts away the sin that He bore; and thus His precious "*blood* cleanseth us from *all* sin," sins of *omission* as well as sins of *commission.* Some seem to think something less or something else than His blood can cleanse from the sin of failing to come up to obey His precepts, while the blood is required only for the sin of actual commission; but sins of omission are as really sin, as sins of commission; and blessed be God, "His blood cleanseth us from ALL sin." And we are justified by His blood as the alone procuring, efficacious, meritorious cause. To nothing else in Scripture is justification attributed as a meritorious cause. "By Him all that believe are justified *from all things*" (Acts xiii. 39).

4th. JUSTIFICATION BY RESURRECTION.—Jesus our Lord "was delivered for our offences, and was raised again for our justification." (Rom. iv. 25). Christ was made sin for us—went into our very place of condemnation under the wrath of God. But God in justice to Him has raised Him out of that place; thus justifying Him, and thus openly preaching to every clime where the fact of His resurrection is known, that the legal barrier between Him and any sinner accepting Christ has been removed. It is not that there is merit or value in the putting away of sin, in Christ's resurrection,—the precious blood alone does that —but there is the exhibition of the satisfaction of God's justice in the finished work of Christ. Christ, on Calvary, added up the penalty demanded, gave Himself as an equivalent, paid thus in equivalent the amount demanded; but God, in raising Christ from the dead, has put to His own hand and receipted the account, so that, not only have we it *paid* by our surety, but *settled* by Him who made the just demand. It was for our offences that He was delivered. It was for our justification He was raised. How entangled are many Christians' ideas of the full meaning of justification is seen in the infrequent use of the resurrection of Christ, which is here so intimately linked with justification. " If Christ be not raised, ye are yet in your sins." (1 Cor. xv. 17); and conversely, "If Christ is raised, ye are not in your sins" His resurrection tells us that God is for us, and that God is for us in consistency, yea, in exhibition of His own majestic justice. So in Rom. x. 6-9, the righteousness of faith speaks thus, " Say not in thine heart, who shall ascend into heaven? (that is to bring Christ down from above); or who shall descend into the deep? (that is to bring up Christ again from the dead);" for the WORD tell us, "that if thou shalt confess with thy mouth the Lord Jesus, and shalt believe in thine heart that God *hath raised Him from the dead*, thou shalt be saved." "Who is he that condemneth?" (Christ most certainly should). "Shall Christ that died, *yea rather* that is risen again." (Rom. viii. 34). "If when we were enemies we were reconciled to God by the death of his Son, *much more*, being reconciled, we shall be saved by His life" (His *resurrection* life) (Rom. v. 10). Thus there is the most intimate and necessary connection between justification and resurrection. The Judge's Son, who took the place, according to the Judge's grace, of the condemned criminal, has shed His blood, but has been raised from the dead, and now stands beyond the forfeit of His life, and the *living* One is the assurance to the condemned one that there is no condemnation. "He was raised *for* (not on account of, but *for*) our justification."

5th. JUSTIFICATION OF LIFE. (Rom. v. 18, Lit.) "As by one offence judgment came upon all men to condemnation, even so by one righteousness, the free gift came (rather to, or towards) all men, unto justification of life." This carries us a step further in the perfect exhibition of the justification of the believer. Not only did Christ come to save, not only did He shed His precious blood, not only did He stand my surety, not only was He raised from the dead as my head and representative, but I am quickened together with Him in this risen life, we are reckoned as having died, and now been raised together with Christ (Eph. ii.) Says the Psalmist, "Enter not into judgment with thy servant: for in Thy sight shall *no* man *living* be justified (Ps. cxliii. 2). As living in the first Adam life, I cannot be justified, but as having died out of the Adam state, and now raised as quickened with Christ. Romans vi. is the full exhibition of this. We do not get justification and acceptance now before God, by restoring to us that which was lost in Adam, but after the penalty has been paid by our surety, and He has been raised, we are, as in Christ, taken out of the old condemnation place, and set down in a new, a resurrection (therefore justified) life, into the very place that Christ now is, in virtue of what He has done. In other words, the old things are entirely blotted out as by the cold hand of the grave. We make an entirely new start, as men that have been dead and are now alive again, living the life of Christ. This is "justification of life." This is the "*newness* of life"—(not freshness, or a merely sanctified walk, but)—life in entirely new circumstances, Christ's resurrection-life, in which we are now to walk, as those who have died ueto sin. So we are called on to "reckon yourselves *to be dead* indeed to sin, but alive unto God, through Jesus Christ our Lord" (Rom. vi. 11); and verse 7, "He that is *dead* is justified (lit.) from sin." It is only as those who have died (in Christ), and who are alive in a life that knows no condemnation (Christ's risen life), that we can say we are justified from sin. This is the bearing of Christ's death and resurrection to our justification *of life*.

Eph. i. 6 tells us that we are "accepted in the Beloved, in whom we have redemption through His blood, the forgiveness of sins." Here we have three things,—forgiveness, redemption, acceptance. We are not yet redeemed by power; but, so far as our sins and their forgiveness are concerned, we do have redemption. And is there One in whom God delights—whom God loves in all His universe? We are accepted in that beloved One—accepted, not on the Adamic state perfected, not

on the angelic state communicated; but accepted in Him who is
the beloved Son, in His resurrection state—quickened with
Him after all the responsibilities of the Adamic state had been
justly met—children in Jesus Christ to God Himself And as
Christ is (not was), so are we in this world. If we continue
our illustration, it will be only to show how surpassing man's
power, is God's justification. Not only has the Judge in His
grace given His Son whose blood was shed, and who was
raised from the dead, but through that risen Son, life is communicated to the condemned criminal, and he takes his place
as a son—not by some gratuitous assumption or temporary
adoption, but by an innate right, having now a son's life, and
hence a son's position. This is "justification of life."

6th. JUSTIFICATION BY FAITH.—"Being justified by faith, we
have peace with God" (Rom. v. 1). Faith is the acceptance of
God's method of justification; faith appropriates what grace
provides; faith apprehends what grace presents. It is not
faith that justifies; but "by grace are ye saved through faith."
All has been finished centuries ago. Faith now gives credence
and credit to the record, and accepts the scheme for the
individual sinner—accepts God's condition of death and resurrection in the Surety, and is thus counted for righteousness,
as apprehending all that God's justice has demanded and
grace has provided. The moment we accept Christ we are
"justified from all things;" we can never be more justified, we
then only begin to grow in grace, but it must be *by faith*, not
by feeling. Many anxious ones are looking for the feeling of
peace within, supposing that to be faith. The experience of
what goes on within me is sense, but is not faith. Faith
believes, not what we feel, but what God says—"He that
believeth not God hath made Him a liar; because he believeth
not the record that God gave of His Son. And this is the
record, that God hath given to us eternal life, and this life is
in His Son" (1 John v. 10). "It is of faith that it might be
of grace." To make it absolutely free and open to any kind
of sinner, no condition was imposed. God comes with a
free gift, and only asks us to accept it. The moment we do,
we have peace (not with ourselves) with God, for Christ is our
peace.

7th. JUSTIFIED BY WORKS (James ii. 24).—Certainly these are
not deeds of the law—" By the deeds of the law there shall no

flesh be justified in His sight" (Rom. iii. 20). They are works of *faith*. (Look at the instances in James,—Abraham's seemed to be against the law of the sixth commandment.) The works of faith show to men that there is faith, the same as the figs on a tree show that the root was a fig root. If a man *say* he has faith— I say to him *show me* your works. (It is not show *God*. He can *see* faith—I can't.) My works justify my faith before men, as my faith justifies myself before God. A Christian is in a low state when he is searching for this faith among his works. He is in a doubtful state when he has to persuade other men that he has faith, who fail to see it in his works. My faith rests on Jesus Christ alone for salvation, and the words concerning Him for the knowledge of salvation. My exhibition to men, of faith, stands on my works of faith alone. The condemned criminal has accepted the terms, the provision of the Judge,—that is, justification by faith. He now lives as the Judge's son, honours the Judge's will, obeys the Judge's commandments, walks, acts, speaks, as becomes the son's place, so that men at once see that he is living in the Judge's home as the Judge's son.

God justifies us, as the author and executor.

Grace justifies us, as the reason in God.

Blood justifies us, as the meritorious cause.

Resurrection justifies us, as God's own assurance.

Life (in resurrection) justifies us, as to our position before God.

Faith justifies us, as the instrument.

Works justify us, as the evidence to others.

CHRIST A PERSONAL SAVIOUR.

" *If a man love me, he will keep my words: and my Father will love him, and we will come unto him, and make our abode with him.*"—JOHN xiv. 23.

" *Lo, I am with you alway.*"—MATTHEW xxviii. 20.

CHRIST A PERSONAL SAVIOUR.

CHRIST *is* a personal Saviour. It is not a *proposition* that saves our soul, but a *person*. It is not in some abstract way that Christ becomes a Saviour to us, but we as persons must have to do with this person—so there is the personality of the *saving* one, and the personality of the *saved* one. We find that in the Apostolic days the apostles never went anywhere, in the exercise of their function of preaching the Word, and preached mere doctrines; they did not preach the atonement, or the extent of the atonement, or the nature of the atonement; they did not tell people even to believe in the atonement, or to believe in something *about* Christ, or to believe in what Christ had done for them; but they went everywhere preaching Christ—Christ a personal Saviour, not a propositional Saviour, not a logical Saviour, but a *personal* one. They did not go in the acute exercise of their powers preaching syllogisms to people, and putting before them premises and conclusions, and saying if such and such is the case, if such and such is the major premise, and such and such the minor premise, and if you put these two premises together, you will reach a syllogistic conclusion, and therefore you have salvation. This might satisfy the schools and the schoolmen; but it does not do when appeals have to be made to the consciences of men. A sinner cannot be brought before his God except individually as a sinner, and through his conscience; nothing of the man is reached until the conscience is reached. I remember well when I was passing through college, and at my being set apart for the ministry, a dear old man whose name I forget, in his charge to us students told us, that as preachers of the Gospel, we should not be content to reach the intellects of men, but that it should be our aim to reach their consciences. But before we reach the conscience, we must first of all see to it that we reach the *tympanum* of the external ear. We can always reach this, if we preach loud enough. Some people don't consider this of much importance, and that mumbling will do. If we have a message from the king to deliver to any person, the first thing we do is to knock at the outer gate or street door; this fitly represents the tympanum of the ear, and we have to get through this first before we can reach the man himself. We find that there are two roads from the outer gate up to the man : the first is, the road by the intellect, and the other road is by his emotions; sometimes I may take the one, and sometimes the other. If I think a man has a good deal of intellect, I will try that road, and aim at convincing his intellect, and so walk up by this avenue to the man—I try to impress the intellect with the truth of my propositions. If on the other hand I find his nature principally emotional I tell him touching stories full of pathos that bring tears to his eyes ; or it may be that I may convince the man by first appealing to the risible faculties. But we must remember that, after you have reached the outer gate of the ear, and have walked up the avenue of the intellect or of the emotions, then, it is only then, you have reached the front door of the man's heart. The conscience has now to be dealt with. The conscience you know is the man. The conscience tells him very humiliating truths; it does not puff him up a bit ; it does not tell you that you are of importance. When quickened before God it tells you your duty—not only that you have not done it, but that you cannot ; it tells you what is right, and what is wrong ; it tells you that you have no power to do right ; it humbles you before God. It is only when the conscience is thus awakened that we have reached the personal sinner, and then we can present to him a personal Saviour— and then what do we do? We retire ! ! !—Because we are not priests but ministers. There is a great difference here, friends. We have a great function. Some people think that the age of pastors, and teachers, and evangelists is gone. Their presence and statements are the greatest proof that it is not. I say this with the greatest amount of confidence. If any man comes to me and says that he does not need a teacher, I say, " My friend, your statement just now is the greatest proof that you do."

I will tell you another kind of twaddle I don't believe in, it is this: when a man comes to me and says that he can get all the instruction he needs from the Bible and that he doesn't want any teacher to instruct him, I don't believe in that at all; it is not true. The chances are that instead of reading the Bible, you will find him busily perusing some monthly periodical. I think that when a man believes he is so clever that he gets everything from the Bible, it is the very germ of Godless independence. We are all dependent, the one upon the other; just as every bone and muscle and every part of our body are inter-dependent, the one upon the other. Think of an independent finger, for instance, trying to move on its own responsibility. We are not a lot of independent balls in a basket; we are not a lot of electrified hairs at the end of a broom. There are three names given to Eve. The first name given to her was Isha, which means "woman from the men." The next, I believe, was the manifestation of Adam's faith. For I believe that Adam is in heaven, and I think we have it in the Old Testament. I believe that he repented, and that is all that ever we have done. I believe that Adam repented and believed the Gospel. He hadn't a big Bible; we have 66 books, he had only one verse, and he believed it all, and he knew it all. He believed all his Bible; it was a very little Bible, but he believed it all. I do not know mine yet. Adam said, "The woman whom thou gavest to be with me, she gave me of the fruit, and I did eat;" and the Lord said, that the seed of the woman was to bruise the head of the serpent, and that life was to spring from her. We find that Adam repents, and believes because of that, and accordingly calls her Hava (or Eve), the mother of all living. It stands recorded in our old Bible that she was no longer to be called Isha but Hava (living), the mother of all living. Adam's faith is implied in the change of name that he gave to Eve. But there is another name that Eve had; it is this, "Male and female created He them, and blessed them, and called their name *Adam*." She was part of the man Adam; she was called Adam with him and in him, *Adam*. "So as the body is one and has many members;" it does not say, "So also is Christ's body," but so also is *the Christ;* so that the body and the head all form together one great eternal unity that through all eternity will show the meaning of God's grace, and God's righteousness, and God's wisdom, and God's

power; with Christ, the head, and we, the members.   Brethren,
let us shun that spirit of independence, and let us cultivate that
disposition to minister unto and to be ministered to by all, and
rejoice if we can by any means communicate a blessing to, or
receive a blessing from, others.   We are *ministers* of the
Gospel of God; we entirely disown all priestly interventions;
we have nothing priestly in our ministry; no priesthood now
but the common priesthood of all believers, and Christ, the
High Priest, and we ministers of the Gospel believe that we are
at one here.   Our work is this: when we get a personal sinner
stripped bare of all his pretences, we have reached his front
door—his conscience, and there knocked; sometimes knocked very loud,—we cannot knock too loud.   Then we bring him
down before the Holy One revealed in all His perfection, the
sinner revealed as he is, stripped of all his pretences, and when
now we have brought them together, we retire; we have no
more to do; we do not go with the sinner in this hand and
God in that, and thus unite them.   No, my friends, we have
no priestly connection between God and the sinner, glory be to
God!   As soon as we bring the sinner and God together we
retire, and say that the work must be done by you two, and we
are nowhere; we retire from the scene.   There is one thing I
would like to say, and that is, that the sinner must be stripped
bare of all his pretences, and brought before God as he is,
and this is the only successful preaching if you want souls
saved; you may lose your character as a preacher; it is the
best thing never to have one.   But we are in for work, business, business.   I know a friend of mine; he is a smart
business man.   I can scarcely see the man during the day on
church work.   When I come into his office, I find his whole
faculties alert in attending to business; he has no time to waste
in talking, it is business, business, with him.   We ministers, I
think, should go in for business; not to make nice sermons,
but to save perishing souls.

I have had considerable experience, when after meetings
were not at all so popular as they are now.   Sometimes we
found when a person was thoroughly in earnest and required
some difficulties to be removed, that a private conversation
did him good.   I very much shocked a friend of mine
by saying that I had not held many after meetings lately.   I
think we may get into canals and forget the rivers.   Many

people seem to be dissatisfied with the ordinary means, with the simple preaching of the Word, and are not content until they arrange for what they call *after meetings*, in which, in my opinion, there seems to me oft-times too much of man's interference; too much seeming additional work to Gospel preaching. Let me not be misunderstood; I do not object to after meetings, but to their abuse. In their proper place they do good, but they must not be regarded as essential, but rather as *incidental.* In my own experience, I have found the best standing cases to be those who have been converted just where they were, and who have had to do with God alone, and whom I have perhaps never seen privately until they have come to profess their faith in Christ, and asked to be admitted to church fellowship. I have found another class of individuals, who through their darkness and sinfulness have come to a personal God, without even a minister coming to help them, and I have found them afterwards calmly, quietly persevering in well-doing, when others chronically required to be flipped up with chronic flips of religious excitement, and pushed on their way by any amount of religious perambulators to carry them up on their way to heaven.

Christ, my dear friends, is a personal Saviour all the way through. Salvation is a many-sided word; it is a blessed word. It is often confounded merely with justification; but it must be remembered that salvation never ends until glorification. There are three aspects in which we may consider it. Why I almost think that in every truth peculiarly divine, there are three aspects to it, and why? Because there is a three-one God. It is a remarkable thing that our discourses often run into three divisions, whether we will or no, and without having any reference to this; of course we all know that it is very convenient, and easily remembered, and so on. We often say that truth has a two-fold aspect; but I am not sure but what it has three. I know salvation has, as distinctly as it can be; a threefold aspect at least; I do not of course exclude any other methods of looking at it. We read of a salvation in the New Testament that is complete to start with, " Receiving the end of your faith, even the salvation of your souls." Faith and the salvation of our souls are here linked together. So the apostle writes, " Unto you who are saved;" he does not say, Unto you who are *going* to be saved. There is a salvation to begin

with, which is spoken of as complete. There is another salvation that we read of, where it says, "Work out your own salvation with fear and trembling,"—work it *out*. Some people mis-
conceive the meaning of this passage; but they forget that before they can work it *out*, God must have wrought it *in*. Paul
here, in effect, says to the Philippians, "You have always been
consulting me as your spiritual father; you have acted well in
my presence; what I wish is that you should be just as good when
I leave you. I am going to leave you, I cannot always be at
Philippi; but God is not going to leave you. Paul is going to
leave you, but God is going to stay with you, and He can carry
on His work without Paul. It is God, my friends, that worketh in you; you cannot have me to consult, but you have God
to work in you both to will and to do of His good pleasure."
Now as to the "fear and trembling,"—let me explain. A man
may take large blocks of granite and he need not be careful in
working at them; but with the diamond polishers it is a very
different thing: they put on their glasses, and take out their
instruments, and with fear and trembling they set about their
delicate work. Now, friends, you are working with diamonds,
not with granite blocks,—with diamonds that are going to shine
in the diadem of Christ for ever and ever. We cannot, therefore, be too careful, friends; we cannot have too much fear,
nor too much trembling—not fear and trembling that I am
going to be lost, but lest the diamond should not come out
nicely edged; lest the gem should not have all the clearness of
the glory of God; lest the nice face should not have the exact
angle. "Work out your own salvation with fear and trembling;" for it is a precious work you have to do; "it is God that
worketh in you both to will and to do of His good pleasure."

We are all delighted with that blessed thought that we are not
left without a friend—a paraclete now. In the second chapter of
1 John, first verse, it reads, "And if any man sin, we have a
paraclete (it is translated, advocate) with the Father." When
Christ was going away He said, "I will send you another
paraclete" (in our translation, comforter). The reason why the
word paraclete is rendered in so many different ways, appears to
me to be because our translators considered the words that they
used expressive of the different functions of the paraclete intended to be conveyed. The meaning of the word *paraclete* is
going along side of. So, my friends, He is one along side of

you to look after your interests—all that you need, whether
comfort or instruction. Sometimes we may require chastise-
ment; well, He can do that. Remember that God is a chastising Father; He does not send us back to the devil to chastise
us; He has a chastising room of His own. The Paraclete is
always with us, to look after our waywardness, and wanderings,
and weaknesses. Christ is a personal Saviour.

There is also an aspect of salvation which is future, entirely
future. "Now is our salvation nearer than when we believed."
And here let me say that we often fall into a confusion of
terms, and confusion of thought, by mingling up things that
differ. Thus there is a salvation completed, a salvation going
on, and a salvation future; if I mingle all these up together,
what a piece of mixed mosaic will I have. If I do not put
things exactly as they are in Scripture, I will get into confusion.
The Old Testament saints looked forward a good deal to these
two salvations being together. They discerned very little
difference between them; it is only since the Gospel light has
come that we have been able by that light to distinguish
between the two aspects of salvation. These Old Testament
saints saw the cross and the crown on the same hill top; we
know that there is a valley between, and that we are treading
that valley; that the cross is behind us, and the crown before
us. They looked forward to the sufferings of Christ and the
glory that should be revealed, as if they were together, and the
salvation they spoke of appeared to them as a unit.

The work of salvation was a gradual and progressive work,
although in one aspect of it, it was instantaneous and complete.
The implanting of the seed is an instantaneous act, but the
growth of the plant is progressive. We are not to be disheartened because we do not see every step of this progress.
God is looking after the bearing of the fruit; God is seeing
that we are growing in grace, and in the knowledge of God our
Saviour, and the more we grow in grace the more will we be
conscious of our own self-insufficiency, of our own *nothingness*.
Young Christians, you know, in their fresh experience feel
like mounting up as with the wings of eagles. I often see them
soaring away to the sun, flying up as on wings of eagles, and
looking down upon us older ones as perhaps somewhat cold
and dead. Well, I don't like to clip their wings: let them
have their time of it, they will be back soon enough. Let

them have their fly; they are mounting up as on wings of eagles;
I do not like to discourage them; I do not like to take a flying
shot and damage their wings; let them have it out, I say.
Just wait a little while; they are flying now, they will soon
want to come back here and *run*.   "They shall run and not be
weary;" this is how our strength is to be renewed, according
to Isaiah.   "They shall *run* and not be weary;" and some of
us know the meaning of that.   Many have run and run a long
while, but weary we have got after all, you know; but grace
will teach us to run and not be weary.   They are running, but wait a little; their pace will shorten by-and-by, and
then they will come to the walking.   "They shall run and not
be weary, and they shall *walk* and not faint;" that is how the
saints renew their strength.   Progress in the divine life is to get
lower down; ambition prompts us to get higher up.   Brethren,
we need to get lower down, lower down.   After mounting up
as on eagle's wings, running and not being weary, walking and
not fainting, having done all in the evil day we are to *stand*.
Stand and meet the foe face to face.   It is then time to learn
the sword exercise; it is time to know how to point and
parry; time to know how to take the enemy at his weak points;
time to know when to strike him.   There is no use attempting
to prove the Bible to an infidel, but the best thing to prove
that it is a sword, is by running him through with it; that will
soon teach him that it is good genuine steel from God's
armoury, then slash away at him, and give him no quarter.
There is no fear, my friends, of the work of the Lord, it is
always getting on well.   Sometimes, you know, He is sowing,
and sometimes reaping; sometimes saving, and sometimes
teaching young souls how to use their swords.   When there is
a little calm, it is time to practice the sword exercise.   Some
people do not know what end of the Bible to take; they use
the sword by the wrong end.   Then, my friends, having learned your sword exercise, when the evil day comes you will not
be able to fly, nor to run, nor even to walk, but having done
all, to *stand*.   There you have the different spiritual exercises,
from the highest flights down to standing face to face, and foot
to foot with the devil, the world and the flesh.   And then after
I have done all I can do, what does the Lord do with me?
After I have stood in the fierce conflict upheld by the power
of His Word, what then?   Oh! my friends, there is some-

thing higher than the active gymnastics. Listen, "He maketh me to lie down in green pastures." Friends, that is the way we are to renew our strength. "To lie down"—mark the position, expressive of our weakness, our passivity, our nothingness. What is a cipher? Some school boy will tell me that its value is nothing, and a million of them raised to the millionth power will only be nothing. Stop, stop a bit; I have a use for nothings. Put the cipher (o) on the corner of a sheet of paper; now put one (1) before it, and what have you? Why, ten (10). And so when I came to Christ, I found I was nothing (o); no mistake about it; but I found that Christ was ten (10) times more valuable to me than ever I had heard Him spoken of, and that He was ten (10) times more precious than I ever could have thought Him. Years rolled on, and I found I was still nothing, and that I had another nothing (o) to add to the sum; but then I found that Christ was 100 times more valuable. Now don't you see the use of nothings, when you have one (1) before them all—the great "One," the Lord Jesus Christ, before all our nothingness. Another year rolled on, and I found I was still nothing, so that I had to add still another cipher; but then, I found that Christ was a thousand (1,000) times more valuable than ever He was before. Now, brethren, we must exalt His name, and sink ourselves in the very dust. As I stand here and think of my own unworthiness and of my utter nothingness, I find I have to add still another cipher; but I can praise His holy name that I can put the glorious ONE before them all, and sing, "He is the chiefest among ten thousand (10,000), and the altogether lovely." Let us add on the nothings, my friends, and we will find that Christ will become more and more precious, and we will sing in the hope of a future salvation, "Our salvation is nearer than when we believed." "To them that look for Him shall He appear the second time without sin unto salvation." I believe that every Christian is looking for Him, whatever his theological notions of the future may be, he is waiting for Christ, the heart is waiting. There may be a difference of thought as to the manner of His coming. I must emphatically denounce the thought that any Christian is not looking for Christ. I am very strong in my thoughts as to the future, but then I don't press them on my brother. In this matter it is the heart and not the head; it is the bride waiting

for the bridegroom ; and to such will He appear "the second
time without sin unto salvation." Then shall we receive the
redemption of the purchased possession, and then shall our
bodies be redeemed. The apostle Paul was waiting for that
on earth, and he is waiting for the same thing in heaven, and
he has not got it yet.

We have salvation perfect to start with ; we have salvation
working out, that we have not yet completed ; and we have
salvation that we are waiting for, when this body of humiliation
will be fashioned like unto Christ's body of glory. "I shall
be satisfied when I awake in His likeness," and not until then.
"Beloved, now are we the sons of God ; and it doth not yet
appear what we shall be ; but we know that when He shall
appear we shall be like Him ; for we shall see Him as He is ;
and every man that hath this hope in Him purifieth himself,
even as He is pure."

Now, brethren, is not Christ a personal Saviour ? I do not
speak of Him as our Saviour, but as my Saviour, and I do not
believe that ever a man who went to his closet burdened with
sin, and knowing himself, and knelt down on his knees before
a holy God and said these two words in reality to Christ, was
ever lost—"My Saviour." But it must be to God, you remember, and it must be genuine, it must be the utterance of
faith. When alone there is little tendency to say it to any
other but God. If any dear anxious soul reads these lines,
let me urge you to go to Jesus Christ yourself ; do not let any
body know ; go yourself, and say, "My Saviour."—"*My*
Saviour." Friends, Christ is a personal Saviour, past, present, and
to come.

NAAMAN THE LEPER.

Now Naaman, captain of the host of the King of Syria, was a great man with his master, and honourable, because by him the Lord had given deliverance unto Syria: he was also a mighty man in valour: but he was a leper."—2 KINGS V. 1.

NAAMAN THE LEPER.

I WOULD call your attention to the fifth chapter of second Kings,—the story of Naaman the Leper.

"Now Naaman, captain of the host of the King of Syria was a great man with his master, and honorable, because by him the Lord had given deliverance unto Syria; he was also a mighty man of valour." He was worthy to be entrusted, bringing glory to the arms of Syria; his career might have been envied by others, if it were not for one damaging word, that had to come alongside of the description of his otherwise great position, and high character and name; a word that carried with it everything that was repulsive and disgusting, especially to the Jew—that was a "*leper.*" The original has it, "He was also a mighty man of valour, a *leper.*" It dashed the whole cup of greatness from his lips, and he stands before a Jew disgusting and repelling. This exactly describes the state of the greatest man on the earth away from God, apart from Christ; it matters not, whether he has got $1,000,000, or $5,000,000, and a great estate, and a splendid house and magnificent equipages; there is one little word that mars it all in the eyes of the Eternal God,—a *sinner.* It matters not what his position, high or low, rich or poor, this word stands against him.

When Nicodemus spoke about being born twice into this world, that would not have helped the matter any; for "that which is born of the flesh is flesh;" it might be rich flesh, but still it would be flesh after all. High or low, rich or poor, the same word is true of all, whatever the adjective may be— a *sinner.* This poor rich man; this small great man; this decrepit Captain who now stands before us, was in the eye of a Jew repulsive and disgusting. Here was a man that had every kind of circumstance in his favor; but what he was, was against him. Sometimes our circumstances may be all that are desirable, but we carry about with us a bane and a curse that makes all our life a gloom and a shadow. His circumstances were all that could be desired from a worldly point of view; but what good did that do him, he was a *leper*. But mark the entire contrast. "The Syrians had gone out by companies and brought away captive out of the land of Israel, a little maid, and she waited on Naaman's wife. And she said unto her mistress, Would God my lord were with the prophet that is in Samaria; for he would recover him of his leprosy."

Look at this little girl, a grand preacher of the gospel; she had not to leave her place to do it; she could preach while in the kitchen where she was; she did not require to go on a platform to do it—no, she could do it in the kitchen. We require more kitchen preaching, as well as more dining-room preaching. Look at the little maid; what a contrast she is to Naaman! She had all circumstances against her; but she carried about in her bosom the secret of healing. All *around* her was against her; but all *in* her was for her. The rich captain had all in his favor around him, but the leprous blood was beating in his heart. The little maid had left her father's home, and her mother's love, and her happy childhood friends, and she was among strangers there; she had become a slave of an alien. But when she sees her master in trouble she forgets all about herself, and remembers that there is living in Samaria a holy prophet of God, who was the representative of God, and had the power of God to heal that which was otherwise incurable, and which in all ages has been incurable. So she says to her mistress, "Would God my lord were with the prophet that is in Samaria; for He would recover him of his leprosy."

There is one striking thought in connection with this story, and that is, how many people God used before that man got cleansed. Why there was first the little maid who set the stone rolling; if it had not been for this private preacher, there would have been no healing at all; she set the whole thing going. A little child can start an avalanche. Then there was the mistress, to whom she spoke on the subject, and then there was one of the servants that had come in while they were talking and had overheard the conversation, who carried it to the King of Syria, and then there was the King of Syria who sent a letter to the King of Israel, and so on all through. There is a great lesson for us here, and it is this. I believe, in my experience as an evangelist, I have found the same to be the case : I cannot point to one individual instance, that I know of, of any one being brought to Christ through my instrumentality alone, where I was the means altogether from beginning to end,—not a single instance ; and I believe that to be the experience of other evangelists ; and the reason seems to be this, that no one should glory but God alone ; and if any of us think that we are to be used exclusively, it would be well for us to read the story of the little maid, and to strive to know the work which God wishes us to do, and then to do it; to know our place, and then to fill it ; to do our work and stick by it, and not encroach on another's work. I believe in individuality of labour—there should be no imitation ; there is nothing more painful than to see one person imitate another in the work of the Lord. We should be willing to be all taught of God, and to do the one work that God would have us do, and then if we work faithfully, we shall have enough to do.

"And one went in and told his lord, saying, Thus and thus said the maid that is of the land of Israel. And the King of Syria said, Go to, go, and I will send a letter unto the King of Israel." There he was wrong ; this little maid talked about the *prophet* in Israel, not the *King* of Israel. But he thought the King must know all about it ; but instead of writing what the girl had said, he wrote down what he thought the girl should have said. And so I find when I have been preaching the word to sinners, people would say afterwards, Do you know what Dr. Mackay said ? and then they would put in what Dr. Mackay should have said.

There is not a more consistent type of sin in the flesh, as corruption, than leprosy, in all the word of God. Medicine in all its departments has advanced very much since that day, but at this moment physicians are as far from finding a cure for leprosy as they were then ; it is as incurable to-day as it was then. In Norway there is a large hospital containing as many as two thousand lepers. Some years ago I had a conversation with the professor who superintended this establishment, and in describing, among other things, the treatment they had there, he gave me some interesting facts concerning this disease.

One fact in particular which he mentioned was this, that the disease of leprosy sometimes apparently attacks the very optic nerve of many of the patients, so that they look at everything with a leprous eye. He showed me some portraits of hideous lepers afflicted with what is called the tubercular kind of leprosy. There were large tubercules upon the face of the men, making them hideous to look upon. He said that if you were to ask some of the lepers in the hospital who were the best looking people in Norway among their acquaintances, they would actually point to some leper more hideous than themselves. The leprosy seems to have taken such hold of their taste for the beautiful that they actually believe that leprosy is beautiful. We may well shudder at such a horrible and hideous thought. And yet young men look upon that fellow who struts about and smokes and drinks and knows all about fast life as a jolly good fellow, and the finest looking fellow in the world. "Oh," they say, "if I could only be like that fellow." What is he? A poor bloated tubercular leper in the sight of the living God; covered with sin and uncleanness "from the crown of the head to the sole of the foot, full of wounds and bruises and putrefying sores."

"And he departed and took with him ten talents of silver, and six thousand pieces of gold, and ten changes of raiment." Yes, he took a good fee with him as if it had been to pay a practicing physician.

"And he brought the letter to the King of Israel, saying, Now when this letter is come unto thee, behold I have therewith sent Naaman my servant to thee that thou mayest recover him of his leprosy." That was a mistake; nobody ever said that the King could do it. The prophet could do it; but the King of Syria could never think of that, and therefore he sent to the King of Israel.

"And it came to pass, when the King of Israel had read the letter, that he rent his clothes and said." He did not know about Elisha. The little maid knew a secret that kings did not know. So it is not with the great and learned that the secret of salvation has ever been. This story shows that God does not use the great, the mighty, and the noble of this world to do His work, but the poor and despised, "that no flesh should glory in His presence." The little maiden knew more than the King of Israel.

He said, "Am I God, to kill and to make alive, that this man doth send unto me to recover a man of his leprosy ? wherefore consider I pray you, and see how he seeketh a quarrel against me. And it was so, when Elisha the man of God." Ah, there was the power, God was there ; He was working through the man. "*The man of God;*" not the King of Israel. If some of you were to take a good concordance and look up those places where the phrase "*man of God*" is used, you would have a good Bible reading. Every Christian is not called a man of God ; he may be considered so in the widest sense, but not specifically so. "And it was so, when Elisha the man of God had heard that the King of Israel had rent his clothes, that he sent to the King, saying, Wherefore hast thou rent thy clothes ? let him come now to me, and he shall know that there is a prophet in Israel. So Naaman came with his horses and with his chariot, and stood at the door of the house of Elisha." He came up in full driving order right away, to show that he had a good team, to show that he was not any poor patient that required to be sent to the dispensary. The prophet, he thought, would come straight out to him ; but no ; we read, "And Elisha sent a messenger unto him." The prophet, I expect, was somewhere, perhaps in a back-room that had very little furniture ; there was not much furniture in those days. This poor man was, perhaps, reading the Law of God, or perhaps was praying ; at any rate he did not think it worth while even to go out himself to see this great captain. I imagine the servant coming in, and saying, "Elisha, there is a grand man at the door; he has a capital pair of horses and a splendid chariot; he appears to have lots of gold and silver and changes of raiment ; he don't look like a leper." Ah, but Elisha knew that the healing did not lie in the *messenger*, but in the *message*. "And Elisha sent a messenger unto him, saying, Go and wash in Jordan seven times, and thy flesh shall come again to thee, and thou shalt be clean."

There are many people who think of the *messenger*, but they forget the *message ;* many people can judge the messenger, but they forget that all the time the message is judging them. I believe if an archangel came here, many of those who had been hearing, would be critics in about five minutes after they had got into the street. I know that it is an easier thing to criticize than to preach. I have found some good critics, but the best

w ty to silence them is to tell them to try the pulpit themselves
tor a Sunday.   We don't profess to be perfect, and if you find
anything crooked in us, the best way is to pray to God and He
will put it right.   Don't mind the *messenger ;* it is the *message*
that you must look at.   When the children of Israel were bitten
with serpents in the wilderness, and Moses set up a serpent of
brass so that whosoever looked upon that brazen serpent would
live and not die, it would have availed them nothing to ' have
talked about it—it was absolutely necessary that they should
look at it in order to live ; it would have done them no good, if
they had even looked at the *pole* upon which the serpent was
raised; to have considered whether it was an oak pole, or maple
pole, or a straight pole, or a crooked pole—no; they must look
at the *serpent.*

If you come here and ask one another, "Did you like that
man or the other man ?" you will go away without receiving
benefit.   My friends, lose sight of every one of us; we are only
poles, and if you have not seen the *Serpent,* we will go away in
self-reproach, crying, "Oh Lord, I took these people's minds
away from the *Serpent ;* they are looking at the character
of the pole."   My friends, do not look at the pole to see
whether it is of Presbyterian, Methodist, Congregational, or
Baptist grain—never mind all that ; what we want you to do
is to look at the serpent on the pole.   We want you to see "no
man save Jesus only."   If you do so, we will go away happy
singing, Hallelujah ! all the way to the glory—till we meet
you in the glory.   Remember that when the sun rises all the
lesser stars are eclipsed.   It is the *message,* not the *messenger.*

"But Naaman was wroth." I like that. I do not like
people to be pleased with my preaching all around: there is
something wrong when that is the case.   I have been preaching
the Gospel now for over twenty years, but I am not at all
satisfied that I have reached the point of successful preaching,
nor do I know of any person that has.   The Gospel is the
power of God to salvation.   The Holy Ghost has given us the
Gospel, and that is the instrument in our hands ; but it is the
Holy Ghost who must drive it home to the sinner's heart.   I
tell my boy, "You hold that chisel straight over that piece of
wood, and I will come down upon it with this heavy hammer."
It is I who supply the power to cleave the wood, all my boy
has to do is to hold the chisel straight.   And that is what I

have to do: I have to hold the chisel straight; sometimes I see
it held to one side, and the result is, that the preaching is un-
successful; it is the straight chisel that is wanted to go deep
down into the sinner's heart through the power of the Holy
Ghost. What I wish is, that my preaching may be so real that,
in such an audience as this, there should be some scene like
this—that (eschewing all attempts at eloquence, but by the
straightforward statement of facts burning into me, and through
me into you, by the Holy Ghost: incarnation facts, crucifixion
facts, resurrection facts, ascension facts; not doctrines even,
not pathos, not rhetoric, not logic, but facts of God, the Holy
Spirit would so use me as an empty vessel, that after I had
finished,)—there would only be two classes in this audience:
one class crying "Hallelujah! Christ is mine and I am His:"
and the other, gnashing their teeth with rage, and thrusting their
fists into my face, crying, "Away with him; it is all lies." This,
I believe, would be the plain result of that kind of preaching.

"And Naaman was wroth, and went away." If I degrade
you (you may be a respectable man in your own esteem) to the
level of a *sinner*, you don't like it, but it is no use getting angry
at me. Suppose a lad came to you with a telegraph message
that contained very unpleasant news: it would be foolish of you
to get into a rage with the boy, he is only the bearer of the
message, and is only waiting to take the answer back. That is
the best telegraph operator that does not alter the message. So,
my friends, I am only an operator; I do not make up the
Gospel, and it is great folly to get angry at me. The Gospel
levels us all down: we have all to take our places in the pit.
Here is a respectable man, who says, "I am a regular sub-
scriber to the cause of Christ, and sit in the Church every
Sunday; I am honest: I pay my debts; I don't profess so
much as that other man, but I would not like to be seen
in his company: he is a great hypocrite, if you only
knew him as well as I do, you would not believe all
his religion." My friends, do you know in England we are
sometimes bothered with counterfeit sovereigns; but I do not
refuse real sovereigns simply because there are counterfeits.
You are comparing yourself with another; "measuring yourselves with yourselves, and comparing yourselves among yourselves." And what does the Apostle say of such? "Ye are
not wise." What is the use of doing it? You are down in the

horrible pit. You are a respectable sinner, perhaps, and you
see a poor fellow trying to get out, and only falling deeper into
the mud; but it's no use going about with a two-foot measure
measuring the depth of the mud. You are not wise to compare
yourselves with yourselves. You know Nicodemus, one of the
most respectable of men, a teacher in Israel, had to be born
again, just the same as the very worst and greatest sinner. And
so it is that God's blessed Gospel levels down all distinctions
and all pretences to self-righteousness.

Some people think they must do something. Like the young
man in the Gospel, who came to Jesus saying, "What shall I
do to inherit eternal life?" He wanted something to do; so
Jesus replied, "Go and keep the commandments." Why did
He not say to him, as He says elsewhere, "Come to me and
I will give you rest?" He did not want rest; he was wanting
to *do* something. The young man told Jesus that he had kept
all the commandments from his youth. But the great Teacher
just put His finger upon the weak spot—*he was very rich*—
"Go and sell that thou hast and give to the poor." By telling
him this, Christ showed him that he had not kept the law, for
the law enjoined in effect that he should love his neighbour as
himself. He did not go over the detailed statement, but showed in the result that he had not kept the law. I have never
yet seen a man that loved his neighbour as well as himself. If
a neighbour's house was burnt down, perhaps he might start a
subscription right off, and not rest satisfied until he could re-
place the furniture, but after coming home from the fire, you
would probably hear him say, "Well I'm thankful it wasn't our
house." The Lord Jesus gave the result, "Sell all that thou
hast and give to the poor." To put this in an algebraic form,
let A equal your neighbour, and B yourself. If B has $100, on
the principle of loving his neighbour as himself, he would give
A $50 if he has none, and retain $50, and if this principle is
still acted upon with other needy neighbours the result will be
that he gives away all that he has, the very result which is in-
dicated in the injunction of the Lord to the young man, and
that would be the result of trying to do the best we can to
meet the Divine requirements.

"But Naaman was wroth, and went away and said, Behold
I thought"—what business had he to *think?* If that man is
going to get his disease cured by the only man in the world

who can cure it, what right has he to *think* anything? He has no right to put in his thoughts at all. So in regard to Divine revelation, you have no right to put in your thoughts: "I will hear what God the Lord will speak"—that is it. A medical friend of mine in Edinburgh had a patient once who wrote him a long letter, in which he gave a very elaborate account of his ailments, and made an appointment to meet him. When he came to his house, he went over the whole story again, and then said, "Doctor, don't you think such and such medicine would do?" "Oh, very well," said the doctor, "there it is, that is what you want." He went away, but he did not get any better. At last he wrote another letter, in which he said, "The last time I wrote to you I told you all about myself, and the medicine I *thought* I should have; but I am no better, so the next time I come I want you to tell me what *you* think, and give me the medicine *you* think I ought to have." That was the proper thing to do. When you go to a doctor it is not for you to prescribe for yourself, you must let him find out the disease and apply the remedy.

Poor Naaman said "*I thought*." He had a nice programme made out, but the prophet's cure had no part in it. He thought "he will surely come out;" but he sent a messenger instead. He thought "that he would come and call upon the name of the Lord his God, and strike his hand over the place, and recover him of his leprosy." So my friends, put away all your *thinkings* and hear what God will speak. Come unto God, not to His angels or ministers, but to God Himself. "Are not Abana and Pharpar, rivers of Damascus, better than all the waters of Israel? May I not wash in them and be clean?" Have I to come all the way from Syria to plunge into that little brook, Jordan? "So he turned, and went away in a rage." There are many of his descendants that do likewise; they turn and go away in a rage, because they are told "there is life in a look at the Crucified One;" they cannot come down to the lost sinner's place, and therefore they never can claim the lost sinner's Saviour. If all the preachers on any platform were asked one after another to give their ideas of the Gospel, I guarantee that I could gather all up in one single sentence, and every minister would say amen to it, however we might differ in doctrine, or in ecclesiastical polity; and it is this,—that there is a CHRIST FOR EVERY SINNER OUT OF HELL,

AND A HELL FOR EVERY SINNER OUT OF CHRIST. This is the
Gospel, state it as you please. Mark you, I said nothing about
the atonement ; nothing about its nature, extent, or application.
It is Christ, a living Christ who was dead and is alive again ; a
Christ for every man, woman and child out of Hell ; a Christ
ready to save.

"And his servants came near and spake unto him, and said,
My father, if the prophet had bid thee do some great thing
wouldest thou not have done it ? how much rather, then when
he saith to thee, Wash and be clean ?" That is common sense,
my friends. And in like manner you are not required to do
some great thing, or to take a long journey, in order to be
saved. God won't give you credit even to the extent of turning of an eye-lash, or lifting a straw to save your souls. It is
"Go and wash and be clean."

> "There is a fountain filled with blood,
>   Drawn from Immanuel's veins ;
> There sinners plunged beneath that flood,
>   Lose all their guilty stains.
> The dying thief rejoiced to see
>   That fountain in his day,
> And there have I, though vile as he,
>   Washed all my sins away."

Try it friends ; you do not get the cleansing before you go,
or *after* you go, it is *when* you go. You are not saved before
believing, or after believing, but *in* believing. The cure is
lying in the water ; the cure is lying in the blood. "Wash and
be clean." There is life and peace in believing. "Believe on
the Lord Jesus Christ and thou shalt be saved."

A friend of mine, many years ago, was told that there was
salvation for any sinner, within the boards of the Bible. It
was said in a rather strange way that led him to believe that he
had only to search and he would find it. He said, "Well,
then, I will have it if it is there." So he began at Genesis and
read all through the first chapter, and he could not see how he
could be saved ; he then read the second chapter, and the
third, and on and on. However, he could not find it. He
read through the whole of Genesis, and he was just as far from it
as ever. He then read Exodus, all about the burnt offerings,
and the sin offerings, etc. All through Leviticus and Numbers
(including the hard names), and in the same way with Deut-

eronomy. He read all through the Pentateuch, and the sub-
sequent books, until at last he came to Isaiah, and when he
was reading the fifty-third chapter, he came across these words,
"By His stripes we are healed;" and then he shut the book
and said, "I have had enough." It does not say, "by His
stripes we may be healed," but "*by His stripes we are healed.*"
This man from that day on became a Christian, and ever since
reading those words he has always taken a special interest in
circulating printed Christian literature as a great means of
spreading God's Gospel.

One word more, and I have done. Some years ago I had
the privilege of addressing about sixteen thousand people in
the Agricultural Hall, in North London, England, after my beloved brother Moody had finished there. At the after
meeting held in the body of the Hall, we had about six to
seven thousand people. I had preached so much that I was
so tired that I left the after meeting to the other helpers there.
As I came down the steps into the street, I saw a young man
coming from the crowd. I saw him just at the side of the
door. As I went out I accompanied a friend on the way to
my lodgings. Turning the street I saw the same young man
again, coming after us. "That young man is following us out
of the anxious room," I said to my friend. "We will soon
find out," I said, "he won't miss us, if he is really anxious."
So we went on until we came opposite the "*Angel,*" a large
brilliantly lighted public house. As I was passing round there,
the traffic was so great, that the young man, I suppose, was
afraid of missing me, so he pressed out of the crowd and came
and tapped me on the shoulder. He asked, "Were you the
man who was preaching in the Agricultural Hall?" "Yes," I
replied. "I want to speak to you." "What have you got to
say?" I asked. He looked somewhat confused, and at last
said, "I really don't know." "Well," I said, "that is rather
hard on me. It reminds me of Daniel and Nebuchadnezzar,
he didn't even get the dream; you won't give me either dream
or the interpretation. But I think I know where to fetch you,
isn't it this? You would like to know whether you are saved
or not?" "Ah, that is it," he said. "That is not very difficult to manage," I said, "If you are really wanting to know,"
"I am indeed anxious to know," he said. I then directed him
to read the sixth verse of the fifty-third chapter of Isaiah. I

repeated the words to him : "*All we, like sheep, have gone astray ;*" "isn't that you friend ?" "Well, that's just me," he said. "Thank God, the battle's half fought and won ; '*we have turned everyone to his own way,*' that's you." "Yes," he said. "Now do you know the last part of that passage ?" "I do not know it." "*And the Lord hath laid on Him the iniquity of us all.*" God does not wait till we lay them. "Now," I said, "go to your room, get on your knees, and open your Bible before you at this passage, with your finger upon it, and repeat every word, every syllable before God, and now, good night." I had to go home to my own people the next day, and the following morning after I had answered my letters, my servant came in and said that a man wanted to see me. I went into the drawing room, and who was it but my friend of Islington, all the way from London to Hull, and he said, "Excuse me, but since you told me to write you, I thought you would not be offended if I called upon you. I came here to see if my soul is rightly saved. There is one thing I want to know in the first place, will that text hold ?" I smiled in his face. "Well," I said, "it has held some pretty big sinners for about twenty centuries, and I do not think you look such a very big weight ; I think it will stand your weight." Then we sat down, and had a Bible reading between two. We read the Bible from eleven until four in the afternoon, he was so anxious to learn. He said he never saw such a text in all his life. Then I told him before he left to go into Moody's anxious meetings, that there was nothing like talking to the anxious. I got letter after letter from him : "I am so enjoying the work among the anxious ;" and "There is no text like Isaiah liii. 6, 'All we like sheep have gone astray.'"

Ah, my friends, this text is open yet, will you take it as you are, and where you are ? If you do, you will never regret it to all eternity. Ah, if you knew the sinner who is speaking to you. If there ever was a sinner deserved hell, it is I, the chief of sinners, but Jesus died for me. We come to plead with you to accept this Christ as your Saviour, "for the Lord hath laid on Him the iniquity of us all."

DEATH AND LIFE.

"For I through the law am dead to the law, that I might live unto God. I am crucified with Christ: nevertheless I live; yet not I, but Christ liveth in me: and the life which I now live in the flesh, I live by the faith of the Son of God, who loved me, and gave himself for me."—GALATIANS. ii. 19, 20.

DEATH AND LIFE.

OUR subject you will find in the epistle of Paul to the Galatians, ii. chapter, 19th verse, "For I through the law am dead to the law, that I might live unto God." What is the chief end of man? "Man's chief end is to glorify God and enjoy Him forever." Here it is more shortly—to live to God. That is the ultimate, the highest thought of man's existence—living to God. What men actually live for since the fall is self—this is the centre, the natural centre of all men born from Adam. It may be sometimes a very vulgar and sensual self, or it may be a very polished and religious self, but it is not so very much the quality of the circumstances that are around that self, as the selfish centre that these circles go around. Man's centre is self. And the true light of God shining upon this world is to show that the highest living and aim of man is to live to God; and that in order to live to God, there must something happen in that man, whatever we may call it—faith, repentance, conversion, new-birth. In fact the Bible has many illustrations, and looks at it from many points, it is in short, a change of centre. Man's centre being self, God comes down to every man, and asks him to change his centre. It is a remarkable thing that when man was under trial, God is spoken of sometimes as repenting. Man was tried from the day of Eden's innocence to the cross of Calvary, for man was not shown in all his iniquity until Calvary; that which showed the greatest love of God also showed the greatest hate of man, for man's history was the history of the gradual development of what was evil in him. We hear a great deal about the development of man. When we go into very suspicious company with some of the would-be developers, they talk about development, in an upward way; they talk about development, I suppose, from oysters up to apes and men; but if we read the history of man, we certainly read of development, but it is all in an opposite direction—it is a development of evil, and not a development of good. It is a degeneration from innocence to evil, and not a growth from savage culture. This is God's teaching concerning the development of man. We find that in Eden, where he was innocent and not knowing any evil, and away from sin, he was so weak and unable to stand, that he sold his God for a bit of fruit. We find that when he had conscience telling him what was right and what was wrong, that he did what was wrong in the face of what he knew to be right, and after sixteen hundred and fifty six years of melancholy history, we find that God pronounces that "every imagination of the thought of his heart is only evil continually," and He had to sweep away the whole of creation, Noah's family excepted, in that flood of judgment.

They say leave a man to his conscience and it will be all right. Will it be all right? My friend, you are about four millenniums too late. God has tried man with his conscience long ago. Men had no Bible from Adam to Moses, but conscience could not tell Noah's sons the theology of the fifth commandment; and conscience could not tell Joseph the theology of the seventh.

God then tried man in the flesh under His law, and it brought out only that man was a transgressor; that the law that he had, he broke, so that if our friend the Rationalist is four millenniums too late, our friend the Ritualist is three millenniums late. God has thus tried man in the flesh, not that God might know, He knew the end from the beginning, but to prove it to men. So when Christ, a person, came, it is no longer merely conscience, and no longer merely law, but it is a person now; and in man's rebellion not only was the mind of the flesh weak in innocence, the mind of the flesh against what was good in conscience, and a trangressor under law, but the mind of the flesh is enmity against God, hates a Person, and hates a Person of God's likeness in the flesh; and the cross of Christ, while showing out all the love of God to the chief of sinners, has shown out all the hate of man against the best God, the glorious God, the God and Father of our

Lord Jesus Christ. They have murdered Him. Oh, brethren, we must not always look at the mere atonement side of the cross, we have also the other side of the cross, which has brought out man's greatest hate and enmity against God.

Now, up to this you may read of God repenting, but from the moment that man was proved to be good for nothing and enmity against God, you never hear of God repenting. God calls upon men everywhere to repent. The repenting is now put upon man. There is no thought of God changing His method of thought, or seeming to do so now, for man is proved at his worst, and man's self is sin—self-seeking carnal self, and he would make all in heaven and earth revolve around himself to serve his own selfish ends. The old astronomers had a strange theory of the motion of the heavenly bodies. They thought that this little earth was so big and mighty that all the heavens revolved around it ; that this little speck of creation that we now know to be so little, was so vast and of such great importance, that the sun went around it, and the planets went around it, and the stars, and all went around our little globe. The erratic motions of planets rather put them out a little. They could not make out for one or two wander-ers that they saw there, still they had to discount these discrep-ancies, and make out that really the whole heaven went around the earth. They never thought that we were one little point revolving around a sun, and that those fixed stars were other suns, possibly with planets revolving around them. We have now reached the true and exact science of modern astronomy, by a change of centre.

Now, unsaved man, you have to get into the God of the Bible, you have not to think that you are the centre, that heaven and earth and men have got to revolve around you, but you have got to find that God is the centre, and that revolving around Him you will get your true place, and you will live to God and not to self. This was the apostle's thought, "That I might live to God." His great aim was, that God might be his centre. Now how did the apostle Paul reach that ? By the words of the text, "I through the law am dead to the law, in order that I might live to God." You see it is not quickly done, you must see one or two things before you change the centre. Before you plan how to govern Canada, you have to be elected governor ; you have to get your seat first, and you

have to do several things.   A man says, "I am bound to live
for God; I am going to live for God."   Not quite so quick, my
friend.   We have something to look into that the apostle Paul
looked into when he said, "I through the law am dead to the
law that I might live unto God."   You have to be a dead man
unto the law in order that, being dead through the law to the
law, you might live to God.   Very shortly, I would just fix
your thought and mind upon this great subject by three words:
first, our condemnation ; secondly, our justification ; and thirdly, our sanctification,

Firstly, condemnation, " I through the law am a dead man ;"
secondly, justification, " I am a dead man to the law ;" thirdly,
sanctification, "that I might live to God."

" I through the law am dead "—that is first.   You must take
the dead sinner's place ; you must know that you have been in
the ditch, before the Samaritan is of any use to you. "They that
are whole need not a physician, but they that are sick."   Go to
any decent man in Toronto that attends church or chapel, and
say, " Friend, are you lost ?"   "Oh, no," he will say, " Not I, I
hope I never shall be.   I am a respectable man ; I have a pew,
two of them perhaps, and I pay my part in connection with
all church doings ; I always have my subscription paid."   "Do
you mean to say that you have never found out that you are
lost."   "Oh, no, not I."   "Well I am sorry for you, you have
to find it out very shortly, ' For Christ came not to call the
righteous, but sinners to repentance.'"   My friend, you have
yet to find out that you are lost.   You have to find out that
the law of God is demanding your death saying ' Die, die.'
Do you feel that you are condemned ?"   "Oh, no, that is a different question."   I think there is rather a confusion in terms.
I will ask him if he feels guilty. and if he says yes, it is all
right.   The condemnation is the sentence of the Judge ; it is
yours to accept the condemnation.   Do you accept this
character that God has given you ?   In this condemnation
that has been pronounced, it is not a matter of our feelings at
all, it is of God's righteous judgment.   Now, friend, are you
prepared to subscribe your name to these lists of sinners, and
say that is the stuff of which you are made ?   I do not ask you
if you feel guilty of all the sins of the first chapter of Romans.
I am sure you are not inclined to murder any one.   The
question is this, will you go by yourself, or occupy the character

as given you? Or, in other words, God has weighed you in
the balance, I give you your weight as God has weighed you,
will you accept it, or go by your own notions? It is more
God glorifying to accept the character there given, though you be
as spotless and blameless as could be. It is more to God's
glory that you subscribe your name, then for the debased
drunkard to accept it. You accept it because God says it; he
accepts it because he has experienced it; you therefore submit
to the righteousness of God, but they "being ignorant of God's
righteousness," have gone about "to establish their own righteousness, and would not submit themselves to the righteousness
of God." Now, here we come to another point, how can God
be just, and justify such a man? Guilty—I have accepted the
doom. Condemned!—I believe it.

How can God be just, and how can I be just with God?
That was the question that rose from the smoke of ten thousand
altars; that was the question that flowed in the blood of
thousands of victims, all raising the question—how can man be
just with God? It is not the question of God's love there, it is
the question of God's justice. How can He be just and yet
let guilty sinners into His presence? Ah! this was the great
question of the Old Testament, answered in the New—How
may God be just, and justify all men who believe in Jesus?

A gentleman came to me at one of my meetings in England
where I was speaking, and said, "I cannot believe in that
Gospel you preach; it is a shocking thing, a shocking Gospel:
do you mean to say that an innocent man dying for a guilty
man is just, or fair, or honest? an innocent man dying for a
guilty man, is it just to the innocent man?" I looked him
straight in the face and said, "No." "Is it just to the guilty
man?" "No." "Then why do you preach it?" I said,
"You may have heard that from some one else, but it is not
my Gospel." "What do you preach sir?" "Listen," I said,
"be very careful what I tell you : my first position is this,
that God became man ; now, sir, where is your logic? In
what system or syllogism do you find that statement, that God
became man? Where is your measuring rod that can measure
that thought? Hast thou scaled the highest heights of
heaven? Hast thou measured the deepest depths of hell?
Dost thou know the comprehension of God? Then tell me
the meaning of God's becoming man? You may reject it or

accept it ; but this you cannot do, you cannot measure it ; you can argue upon it ; you can only accept or reject it as a revelation from God. And my second is like unto my first, the Gospel that I preach is this, that God became man and put away sin by the sacrifice of Himself. Can you tell me the meaning of ' putting away sin by the sacrifice of Himself?' I cannot, cannot comprehend that." Blessed be God ! the simplest child in this meeting can apprehend it. It is one thing to comprehend a thing, and another thing to apprehend it, and if the well is deep, yea, bottomless and fathomless, that well of His Gospel is full and running over, and the child's little tumbler can be filled, as the well is full to the brim. God became man and put away sin by the sacrifice of Himself ; that is God's Gospel, that is the Gospel in the New Testament, that is the Gospel of Revelation, that is the Gospel to the glory of God.

Darius loved Daniel; the advisers of Darius were jealous of Daniel ; they entrapped Darius into making a rash decree in order that they might entrap Daniel ; Darius could not fall back from his word ; Daniel had to go away to the lions' den. Darius might have gone all day long endeavouring to get Daniel off, but his love could not do it, his mercy could not do it, and his pity could not get Daniel off ; he might have gone to the council, but they would have said, " The law cannot be broken." The law came in at every point. He could not let him off. He might scheme from the rising of the sun to the going down thereof, but the grace, and the love, and the mercy, and the pity were of no avail, because there was the law—the law, righteous or unrighteous, the fixed law of the Medes and Persians, standing dead between Darius and Daniel, and he must away to the lions' den. He went—the law of the Medes and Persians had done its worst. They take him away to the den of lions, and I have often thought that when Daniel sat that night with the lions' mouths graciously stopped, he could look up to the mouth of the den and say, " Well, you have done your worst now, what more can you do? I, through the law, am dead ; but I am more now, I am dead to your law : you cannot put me in again." And then, next morning, when Darius came to him and said, "Daniel, Daniel, has God delivered you ? " " Yes, I am here," and he could then live as the brightest specimen of the righteousness of Darius in all the kingdom of the Medes and Persians. I, through God's law, in my substitute, am a dead man to the law, that I might live unto God. I have death and doom behind me, and nothing before me but the blessed hope of the return of my Lord. " I through the law am dead to the law, that I might live to God. I have been crucified with Christ, nevertheless I live no longer, but Christ liveth in me."

If you take the lost sinner's place, what does God say to you, my friends? I can do nothing but save you. Let Him save you. You will forget your unworthiness when you are in the embrace of your Heavenly Father, as did the prodigal son.

THE ACCEPTABLE SACRIFICE.

" *I beseech you therefore, brethren, by the mercies of God, that ye present your bodies a living sacrifice, holy, acceptable unto God, which is your reasonable service.*"—ROMANS. xii. 1.

THE ACCEPTABLE SACRIFICE.

THE special aspect of truth before us is, "Our bodies are to be presented as a living sacrifice, holy, acceptable unto God, which is our reasonable service." God is wanting service from us, and sacrifice. The sacrifice is characterized as being living. It is not a dead animal put upon an altar. It is a living man, living to God. It is a living sacrifice. It is wholly separated by God himself— by His own sanctifying act, unto the Lord. It is acceptable to the Lord, who is seeking workers, worshipers, witnesses; and in the person of the redeemed sinner, sanctified and consecrated unto Him, we have a holy worshiper, a true worker, and a consecrated witness—a priest, a Levite, and Nazarite. And it is our "reasonable service," not the irrationalism of mere externalism, and attitude and action of the body, but that which proceeds from that internal mind that God has given, a reasonable service—reasonable as being holy, and in being acceptable unto God, and reasonable as being sent up to God by the whole man. Our body is presented to God as a casket which contains the priceless gems. We find the Lord Jesus spoken of as tabernacling here in the flesh. So we have this tabernacle, the body, which contains in it the holy place and the most holy, which are to be given up entirely to God for His work, for His worship, and for His witness.

This is all founded, you will see, with the greatest, because the Divine caution, that this is no legal sanctification, no legal consecration, no act or profession of holy service as Israel gave on the Mount, when they did not know their own weakness, when the Lord came down to prove them, and they said, with the confidence of the flesh, "All things that are written, we will do." They had the intention to do it, no doubt, at the time, but they had not the power; and this is why fallen humanity, sprung from Adam, must always be a liar. "Let God be true, and every man a liar," springs from the necessities of the case of fallen humanity, because fallen humanity will strongly promise to do what it has not the power to do, as revealed in God's Word—without strength, but still with the presumption of promise.

It is not, then, the offering of legalism, in the strength of the flesh, that we are asked to present our bodies, living, holy, acceptable sacrifices unto God; but as those who have known and experienced the mercies of God, for it is by them we are besought. "I beseech you, therefore, by the mercies of God" —the mercies of God as revealed fully in the whole sweep of doctrine taught in the Epistle to the Romans up to this point. In the divine settling of every question that has arisen, or may arise, concerning the standing, the state, the position, the guilt, the innate corruption, of every sinner born from Adam—when every question has been raised, in the wisdom of God every question has been met by the grace of God according to the righteousness of God; and His grace and His righteousness have thus both been united by His eternal wisdom. His infinite grace, and infinite righteousness seem to be in opposition, so far as we poor, guilty, weak sinners were concerned; but infinite wisdom came welding these together, so that grace reigns now through righteousness, and God can be just and the Justifier of him that believeth on Jesus, when His love is thus seen flowing down free and full as a river, bringing pardon, and peace, and joy, giving us those grand hallelujah choruses —songs of God, as seen in chapters five to eight of this glorious epistle—giving us peace with God through our Lord Jesus Christ—giving us access into that grace wherein we stand—giving us to rejoice in the hope of the coming glory; and if the glory should be a little distant, even to give us to "glory in tribulation also, knowing that tribulation worketh patience, and patience, experience, and experience, hope." Also the very love of God is shed abroad in our hearts. And our final salvation depending on His life in resurrection, we thus can make our boast in God Himself.

These are some of the mercies, as far as the question of our sins is concerned, that are at the foundation of all our consecration; and when we come to the question of our sin—or what we are, as contrasted with what we have done, we find all full of mercies; no condemnation to them that are in Christ, and God Himself dwelling in us; and God Himself standing for us. "And if God be for us, who can be against us?" Now with all the mercies of God thus poured out upon us, chief of sinners among the Gentiles, or among the Jews, with a revelation from God, or without a revelation from God, wandering far from Him, the worst and the vilest of men, provided for according to the righteous requirements of God, everything is settled in the past, everything settled in the present, everything settled for the future; what more befitting than to come in now. "I beseech you, brethren, (by those mercies,) that ye present your bodies a living sacrifice, holy and acceptable to God."

I think it will be profitable to look in the first place, at the God-ward side of this truth, because, if there was no God-ward aspect of this consecration, there could be no man-ward. God is the beginning, and God brings in the beginning; and on the foundation of what God is, and what God has done, and how God has done it, we are called upon to present our bodies to Him. And these two lines of truth you will find in the grand old picture book of the Bible, namely the Old Testament.

Little children—and this we are taught to be in simplicity in learning our Father's will—are often taught by pictures. Just as little boys are much more interested in pictures, than merely dry doctrinal teaching, so the Lord has graciously given us a picture book.

You remember when Nicodemus could not understand the new birth, the Lord Jesus took him away to the picture book of the Bible, and showed him a serpent lifted up, and said, "There is where eternal life is to be secured." Ah! friends, we are safe when we use our Old Testament as Christ used it. The enemy is trying, on all sides, to take away our Old Testament from us—our grand old Bible, with Moses, and the Prophets, and the Psalms; but we are all safe when we keep by Christ's use of them, as he used them reverently and fulfilled them to the letter, and used them defensively against all the temptations of Satan. It is very remarkable to note the use that Christ made of the Old Testament in His conquering of Satan—fulfilling the word of prophecy, "By the words of Thy lips I have kept me from the paths of the destroyer ;" and that these words were taken from the Book of Deuteronomy, the very book that the enemy now most savagely assails, and that the Lord Jesus Himself used this book in the act of defence against the fiery darts of the enemy.

We go back to the picture book, and there you find two pictures, one in Leviticus, and the other in Numbers. In Lev. viii. you have the divine consecration of the Priest and Levite. In Numb. vi. you have the self-consecration of the Nazarite, and all this must be taken into account in connection with the truth of this subject, else we will not have an all-sided view of the method of Divine consecration. All through there is a rotundity about truth. We are so apt to look upon truth from one point of view, and to be carried away by that; but we are told to walk about Zion, and go round the high towers thereof, to consider her palaces and mark her bulwarks well. We are to go round Zion. We are to go round all the revelation that God has given. So if God consecrates the priest and Levite on the one side, the Nazarite consecrates himself to God on the other: and in the priest we have the worshiper consecrated to God; in the Levite we have the worker; and in the Nazarite we have the witness. The separated witness, the active worker, the holy worshiper, are the three thoughts that we have in the picture book that God has given us in connection with the history of Israel.

Let us look then at the first, as contained in the first twelve verses of the eighth chapter of the book of Leviticus. When we get Aaron in the priesthood, he stands before us as the great type of Christ. Aaron alone represents Christ alone. Aaron and his sons represents Christ and the Church. When we get Aaron and Moses, we have Priest and Prophet. Moses, Aaron, and the elders, as seen in Lev. ix., point to Christ as Prophet, Priest, and King, on the eighth day (the Millennial scene).

We have the same questions raised as are raised in Rom iii. and v., and met by the figure here, and by types and illustrations, as we have them met doctrinally in the Epistle to the Romans.

We have the ram of consecration; we have the basket of consecration; and we have the days of consecration now brought before us in Lev. viii. And these are to be before us as the priests and Levites of the Lord. Verse 12 shows us Aaron getting the oil poured on him without any blood : Christ required no sin-offering before the Holy Ghost fell on Him without measure. But when we come to the sons of Aaron, there is no consecration until sin-offering and burnt-offering have been presented.

In verses 12 to 21, we see not only is the sin-bearer identified with all the guilt of the sinner; but the sinner is identified with all the worth of the victim. All the worth of the preciousness of Christ is ours, as all the guilt that we had was His. It was a burnt sacrifice of a sweet savour, and the offering made by fire unto the Lord, as the Lord commanded Moses. Here we have the sin-offering and the burnt-offering presented before there is a word of the consecration of the sons of Aaron. Then after the whole question of sin and acceptance were met in the sin-offering and burnt-offering that were presented, we read: "Aaron and his sons laid their hands upon the head of the bullock for the sin-offering." This was the Eastern method of identification, in which the sinner came confessing his sins; and the sin-offering was identified with all the sin of the offerer, the offerer identified with all the value of the burnt-offering.

" And he slew it; and Moses took of the blood of it, and put it upon the tip of Aaron's right ear, and upon the thumb of his right hand, and upon the great toe of his right foot." (Lev. viii. 23.) Here is the blood before the oil, and in the blood we have the life taken. The blood in Scripture is never spoken of as coursing through the arteries of the living victim. It is not the life in the victim, but it is the shedding of blood: "Without shedding of blood there is no remission." The perfect and co-equal with God, comes in the strength of His own love, and the power of His own holiness; and we can be anointed with the Spirit of the living God, for the service which he is to undertake. And when the anointing oil is poured upon Aaron's head, God separated him for the work. He sanctified him. We will never get into the full idea of consecration until we see it in the aspect of separation—separation from, and separation to. Its use is very wide in the Old Testament—separation from, and to all things concerned.

The Spirit of the Lord could be given to Christ without measure, for "He was holy, and harmless, and undefiled, and separate from sinners." The perfect moral glory of the Lord Jesus, His entire separation from all that was of this world of sin, is thus shown forth. He stood there and heard the voice

of God, and received the anointing of the Holy Ghost. When
He stood there, and the voice was heard, and the dove rested
upon Him—"This is My beloved Son, in whom I am well
pleased"—no sacrifice did He require for Himself. Hence He
is the uncreated One—the all-creating One; because if any creature had laid down his life at the command of God, he had nothing to spare to transfer to another, because God had given him
his life, and could, in justice, at any time demand it. Christ is
separated with His own as brethren, just as Aaron and his sons
together were consecrated with blood. In verses 22 and 23,
we have the whole body a living sacrifice consecrated by the act
of God, through His prophet—by the act of God, to the Lord.
And this is the fundamental truth of it all, and what makes the
other a natural sequent. When I realize I am not my own,
but am bought with a price, and the blood of consecration is
upon my ear, and the blood of consecration is upon my hand,
and the blood of consecration is upon my foot, and the whole
man, from head to foot, his whole spirit, his whole soul, his
whole body—all that the man is—his mind, his will, his affec-
tions, everything that the body contains, as the tabernacle containing all the preciousness of the gold and glory—all by the
act of God, by the blood of consecration separated to God,—
what manner of persons ought we to be? This truth, in connection with the Christian's walk, should have the greatest
power upon everyone of us—what the Lord has done—not so
much what I am to do—that follows, but what the Lord has
done. If the *blood* of consecration is upon that hand by a
Divine act, dare that hand do anything that is against or in-
consistent with that precious One whose blood was shed?
Would that not carry a consecrated hand into all business? I
have sometimes been asked by some Christians about this secular call, and the other secular call. "My friend," I say, "if a
consecrated hand is put to anything, that call becomes immediately consecrated." It is a sacred hand, and the carpenter with
his saw, or plane, or chisel, imitating the carpenter of Nazareth,
is going forth as a royal priest with a consecrated hand to provide things that are honest in the sight of all men, and laboring
and working with his hands the thing that is good, that he may
have to give to him that needeth. And thus the consecrated
priest, let him be preacher, or carpenter, or mechanic, wherever he may go, he caries a consecrated hand right into every

part of his work. Then shall we find the exhortation of Paul, concerning consecration, to be consistent with servants obeying their masters, whether converted or unconverted : "Not with eye-service as men-pleasers, for ye serve the Lord Christ." It is with a consecrated hand, by the blood of the consecrated ram, that thus we go forward to the business of the world. This is very practical ; this goes down to the business, to the counter, to the shop, to the office. If this were known and practiced, such a hand could lift no pen to write a name, but what would be for the glory of that blood shed. We would find more practical testimony for the Lord among those who profess His name. We would hear of no Christian being involved in suspicious things in the world's business, if he carried the consecrated hand into the city, and into all his business ; and if there was a doubt about any line of conduct, he would say, "But that hand is consecrated with the blood of consecration ; I am holy to the Lord." And only holy communications would be received by the ear ; because it is holy to the Lord. If we realized more that we had consecrated ears, the revelation of God would come into us much more simply than it does. We would find fewer difficulties among Christians about interpretations of the Word of God, if we all realized that we approach that Book with the blood of sprinkling, and come to listen, as holy priests, to the voice and communication of the living God, with the blood of consecration marked upon us. Then my foot—shall it tread in paths that would not become a consecrated foot ? Do you ask me to go here or there ? I go at once, if the blood-touched foot can go. We go at once if we can carry our Christ as slain, and rejected, and murdered by this world. Then we can go, knowing that the blood of consecration is upon the foot, and ear, and hand—the living man thus consecrated to the Lord. This blood that we have here is the measure of our consecration. "Ye have not resisted into blood." How much must I seek to do for the Lord ? Love my neighbor as myself ? A little further—what ? To love one another as Christ loved us. And how far ? To lay down our lives for the brethren, for we are consecrated by blood, and until we have gone on to the full measure of it, we are short of what the consecrated One has done.

If in the service of the Lord my ear has to be taken from me, and my right hand taken off, and I have to lose my right foot, I am doing nothing more than I have been consecrated for. We have been consecrated by the blood mark upon us, and as Queen Victoria's troops know how to charge at the word of command, but never to reason why, though they go into the Valley of Death, so the soldiers of the Lord Jesus, consecrated with blood, go forward, calmly but resolutely, to fight, with the oath of consecration on the ear, on the foot, and on the hand, crying, "Life, life is the measure of my consecration to the Lord, consecrated by the blood." Well might he say, "Who is sufficient for these things?" It is enough to dishearten a poor struggling one down here when we see such a great ideal before us; but God will never bring down the ideal to our level. He will raise our level up to His ideal. We are predestinated to be conformed to the image of His Son, and He will never be satisfied till we are so, and we shall never be satisfied till we wake in His likeness. God puts the consecration of Christ unto the death as the point at which we are to aim. He does not tell me to follow Paul, or Abraham, or any other saint. Ah! we are always aiming at lower models and saying, "I wish I were like Mr. So-and-so." My friends, all the mirrors on earth have cracks across them, and the cracks are reflected when we take the reflected light from them; and just as often as reflection goes from mirror to mirror upon earth, we imitate, it may be, even the flaws, while we forget the beauties. Let us go straight to the Lord Himself, and see the measure of His consecration. But if we have the measure of it in the blood, we have also the power of it in the oil of consecration. Moses took of the anointing oil, and of the blood which is upon the altar, and sprinkled it upon Aaron and upon his garments. If I am told to clear away a mountain, I have not the power to do it, and it is to me an impossible thing; but if I get sufficient engines and men, it then can be done. If I am told I am to be consecrated unto the death, I may say, "Who is sufficient for these things?" But God has provided His Spirit, that will not rest within us, but feed us by the truth of God, until we are in the likeness of Jesus. "When He shall appear we shall be like Him, for we shall see Him as He is; and everyone that hath this hope in HIM purifieth himself even as He is pure;" and as the blood tells us of the measure of our consecration as the priests of God, so the oil tells us of the power that God has given to enable us to rise up to this ideal. And it is by the indwelling Spirit of God, ungrieved and unhindered, and the activities of His work within us, that we go onward, calmly and surely imitating the Lord, and going forward in the path that He has trod, raising within us those holy aspirations and those holy determinations now to live wholly, and unreservedly for Him. It is by the oil of the Spirit of God giving the power within, that now we live in the path of priests.

I need not explain that every child of God is a priest of God. All children of the living God now are as the sons of Aaron, for "He hath made us unto our God kings and priests." Meantime we exercise our functions as priests in interceding for others around us. By and by, in the glory to come, there will be the manifesting of the royal priesthood, of the glory of the Lord. But if you turn to Peter, you will find two things spoken of as to our priesthood,—we are a *holy* and a *royal* priesthood. We manifest what Christ is, within as before God, and without us in the world at large. As the first of these, "Ye are also a *holy* priesthood to offer up spiritual sacrifices acceptable to God by Jesus Christ;" and at the 9th verse, as to the second, "But ye are a chosen generation, a *royal* priesthood, an holy nation, a peculiar people, that ye should show forth the praises of Him who hath called you out of darkness into His marvellous light." The two aspects of our priesthood, as they are within the veil and outside in the world, are these : *holy* to offer sacrifices, *royal* to spread out here in a royal way to the world at large, the praises of Him.

Are we acting as a royal priesthood? Do we act as the great ambassadors from God? Have we spread the testimony of the Lord Jesus as a royal priesthood to the ends of the earth? Have we satisfied our consciences and gone like kings with the embassy of God? An ambassador carries with him the honour of his country. Have we come down from the height of our glory and sounded the proclamation "over vale and hill"? I am glad to see that one phase of Christian work is getting popular—the missionary aspect—but we are truly guilty in this matter. We talk about consecration, and about being the Lord's, but what are we doing? "Ye shall be witnesses unto me both in Jerusalem, and in all Judea, and in Samaria, and unto the uttermost parts of the earth;" and millions of people have never heard there is a Christ for them, or that there is a salvation from

God.   We have all fallen from the height of our royal priesthood
by not going outward to these lost brethren. The history of Missions in the present day is only about one hundred years old.
Seventeen centuries have elapsed, and Christians thought their
fellow-Christians mad when they tried to rise up to the height
of their obedience and of their responsibility in this matter.
If Queen Victoria desired a proclamation sounded through all
the world, how long would it be before that proclamation would
be known, with the machinery—the Army, the Navy, the
Exchequer—that would be set in motion to issue it? Would
it take eighteen centuries? Rather let me say it would take
eighteen months. The proclamation, as the little hymn says,
would be, "sounded over vale and hill." What is the command,
and what are our resources? All the power of the British Navy,
the British Army, and the British Exchequer? No. "All power
is given to Me in Heaven and on earth." What for? "Go ye
therefore into all the world and preach the Gospel to every
creature." And then? "Lo, I am with you." I think that
gives us a good hint; this has been the mistake of the dispensation.   Christians have been trying to get universal conversion
instead of universal evangelizaton. That is the mistake; that
is at the root of it all. Instead of obeying the Lord's command
and giving the whole world a chance, we have been high-farming
little corners, and setting workers down so closely as to interfere
with each other's work, and the poor heathen lying in their
heathenism and godlessness. Let our hearts be burdened to
begin with, and our prayers rise up, and our money stream forth,
and our young men be told that the great crown for the worker
is the foreign field, and that the great call of the day is to stand
up in obedience to the Lord, and to go forth in His name, to
tell the gospel of peace through the nations of the earth. For
it is not written: "Lo! you will be successful; lo! you will get
the whole world laid at your feet; lo! every one will receive
you; lo! every nation will turn to you." No, no; but, "Lo!
you will find that it is hard work gathering out the net from the
sea." It is not the abundance of the sea, yet it is the netful out
of it, and you will find that you will need to go to Him very
often, for it will be hard work : "Lo! men will all believe you."
No, no; but, "Lo! I am with you alway, even to the end of
the age." And this is the practical outcome of our consecration
to Him,—the obedience that would depend upon that promise.

It is lying there for faith to act upon it. All power in heaven and earth has been lying there for eighteen centuries. Shall we not rise up and take hold of it, and get our souls burdened, and see wherein we are guilty each in this matter.

But we must pass on. There is the *basket* of consecration. Some do not attend much to this : " And there eat it with the bread that is in the basket of consecration." We see this perfectly in the Lord Jesus. When His disciples went to buy bread, He said, " I have meat to eat that ye know not of." And what was His meat? Doing His Father's will. And here it is in the basket of consecration. It is finding the will of God and knowing it, and doing it, that we are thus fed day by day. The morning's blessing will not do for the evening, and the manna of yesterday will not do for to-day ; but the bread of the basket of consecration must be partaken of day by day. thus we have to say, " Give us this day our daily bread."

And last of all ; " Ye shall not go out of the door of the tabernacle of the congregation in seven days until the *days* of your consecration be at an end. . . . Therefore shall ye abide at the door of the tabernacle, and keep the charge of the Lord as He hath commanded." Here is our attitude now as those who are waiting for God's Son from Heaven. We are to abide all the days of our consecration—that is, until the Lord comes, and takes us into His own presence. And what are we doing? Keeping the charge of the Lord, the charge that He hath given us, turned to serve and wait. And we are waiting here in obedience to His command as the waiting and working ones—waiting for Him to return. And to see the glory that we have mirrored forth in the ninth chapter, going forward in the power of His glorious truth, and in the energy of His mighty Spirit, keeping that charge, doing His will. Thus we shall be in that frame that the Nazarite was in, which I refer you to at your leisure in Numb. vi.; consecrating himself, laying himself down, all that he has and is, for the Lord. So now we are not living as men who shut themselves out from the world, and separate themselves from its midst, but living as men to bear the testimony of the Lord, to fight the battles of the Lord. Thus separated by God Himself, acceptable to Him as workers, worshippers, and witnesses, the only thing that as rational men we can do, is to present ourselves to the Lord, and no reserves. What else do we live

for but this? We are fools if we live for anything else. We
are throwing away the very existence that God has given us.
And when I look upon the mass of men, the great majority
of whom, I believe, are professing that blessed name that is being trampled upon by the world; when I behold that open infidelity, and that certain kind of Christianity that professes the
name, but has not the reality, I think of the potential energy
there is with us, if we could only rise up to the dignity of our
sonship, and be holy, and acceptable, and consecrated, to the
Lord—not a part of our being, not a little part of our time, but
entirely. Realizing what the Lord has made me, I fall into
His way, and I say, "Yes, Lord, this goes with my whole soul
and mind." "What shall we then say to these things?" It is
a beautiful thought, putting our hand into Christ's; and it reminds me also—of these warlike customs in the days of
old Rome, when the *sacramentum*, or oath, was given to the
soldiers. The leader of the detachment that was to be sworn
to live and die for the Senate and the people of Rome, read over
at large the *sacramentum*, and then the right hand man held up
his right hand, and repeated the Latin words, "*Idem in me*"
("The same for me"). And down it went, till the last left hand
man held up his right hand in what he thought the most holy
attitude, and swore the same oath. And the Apostle says, "What
shall we say to these things?" Are we ready to hold up our
right hand to him, each individual of us, and cry, "*Idem in
me*," ("the same for me") and to pass along the lines the shout
of praise and glory, to sing as we go on like a mighty host
unto the Lord, filled with His Spirit, and sublimated, sanctified
and purified, made more and more like to Him, transformed
into His image, joying in His mercies, humbled with our fail-
ures, glorying in His grace, glorying in what He is, not even in
what Christ has made us. Let us not glory even in that our
names are high up in heaven's list yonder, and that we are
strong before the Lord; but rather glory in the grace that has
put us there, and in the God of grace that has made us what
we are in Christ; for we make our boast in God.

THE ACCEPTABLE WILL OF GOD.

" *I beseech you therefore, brethren, by the mercies of God, that ye present your bodies a living sacrifice, holy, acceptable unto God, which is your reasonable service. And be not conformed to this world ; but be ye transformed by the renewing of your mind, that ye may prove what is that good, and acceptable, and perfect will of God.*"—ROMANS xii. 1, 2.

THE ACCEPTABLE WILL OF GOD.

"I BESEECH you, therefore, by the mercies of God." The mercies of God have been explained in the Epistle already, but I draw your attention to this "therefore." "I beseech you, *therefore*." Sometimes, as you know, the division into chapters breaks the continuity of the teaching; and we shall go back, therefore, a verse or two, to link on the former teaching in the end of the eleventh chapter of Romans, with the teaching now before us. "Oh the depth of the riches both of the wisdom and knowledge of God! How unsearchable are His judgments, and His ways past finding out!" And if poor, ignorant man would take a lesson from this, he would not try to measure the infinite by the finite; "for who hath known the mind of the Lord? or who hath been His counsellor? Or who hath first given to Him, and it shall be recompensed unto him again? For *of* Him, and *through* Him, and *to* Him are all things: to whom be glory for ever." There is the *highest ideal* of God in the creature—"Of Him, and through Him, and to Him are all things: to whom be glory." From Him, through Him, and back to Him, and glory to Him. "I beseech you *therefore*," immediately coming after this wonderfully comprehensive statement, "Of Him, through Him, and to Him are all things: to whom be glory for ever." "I beseech you, therefore, brethren, by the mercies of God, that ye present your bodies a living sacrifice, holy, acceptable unto God, which is your reasonable service." Since the highest ideal that we, intelligent, fallen, and now saved beings, have of being entirely in the mind of God is, "Of Him, and through Him, and to Him, are all things," and glory in all—from eternity, through time, to eternity again; from His counsels, through the manifestations of the activities of His grace, on to the final triumphs in glory yonder—we receive the exhortation with all its force, "I beseech you therefore"—and this is the way we should aim at reaching the highest ideal—"that ye present your bodies a living sacrifice, holy, acceptable unto God, which is your reasonable service. And be not conformed to this world; but be ye transformed by the renewing of your mind, that ye may prove what is that good, and acceptable, and perfect will of God. For I say, through the grace given unto me, to every man that is among you, not to think of himself more highly than he ought to think; but to think soberly, according as God that dealt to every man the measure of faith." There, in what comes after the exhortation, we have what is to be cultivated, in order that that ideal, being before us, may be produced in us and by us in our education down here, as being educated for the eternity that is to stretch on before us. Here we get as essentials for rising up to this thought, "Of Him, to Him, and through Him are all things: unto Him be glory."

We have, in the first place, devotedness, *thorough devotedness* of the whole man, and no reservation, nothing kept, the whole burnt-offering upon the altar, the living sacrifice ; then obedience, *unquestioning obedience ;* and with this unquestioning obedience the deepest spirit of *humility* and *dependence ;* for if we have the devotedness and the obedience, we have an indication and proof of the will of God, essentially good and perfect, leaving nothing out. We have reached the terminus of it, and it is "well pleasing" (the same word used as that about the sacrifice). For devotedness, thorough devotedness, and unquestioning obedience precede this proving, and we find that it is obtained in the spirit that follows—"Through the grace given unto me ; to every man that is among you, not to think of himself *more highly* than he ought to think ; but to think soberly, according as God hath dealt to every man the *measure of faith." Humility* as to the place that he has, and the walk to which he is called, and *dependence* upon the Sovereign God, who gives as He wills.

Do not let us boast of the place that grace has given us, but let us boast of the grace that has given us the place ; not taken up with being even seated in the heavenly places in Christ, but worshipping Him on the throne, whose grace has set us there

—every eye thus turned to the God of grace that set us upon the throne. Ah! "Let us not think more highly than we ought to think," but, in utter humility and daily dependence, live the life that God has been calling men to, during these six millenniums—the manifestation of creatures thoroughly depending on Him for every breath, and so lost in His will, that they have no wills of their own; not in innocence, and not in ignorance, but in righteousness and truth. Man has fallen from innocence, and God, making the wrath of man to praise Him, has raised him to a higher level in righteousness, holiness, and truth. Not in ignorance, as the stars of night, and the creation around us, which obey the will of God. When we say, "Thy will be done," we may look abroad to the stars of night, and we see the planets circling round the centre of light and heat, and they are all doing the will of God; even the erratic comets, stretching out their wide paths, are fulfilling His will, the stars of the universe are doing His will, and the blades of grass that spring up in our path are doing His will, and the flowers that burst open on a spring day, and the summer fruits of nature, and the rushing river, and the rolling ocean, and the thunderstorm, and the lightning, are all His messengers in nature, are all doing His will. He could, when He was here on earth, speak to those waves of the Sea of Galilee, and they would listen to His voice, and do His will, as has been beautifully said.—

> "Calmly He rose, with sovereign will,
> And hushed the waves to rest;
> 'Ye waves,' He whispered, 'Peace! be still!'
> And they calmed like a pardoned breast."

It is not as ignorant nature, but as men made in the image of God, the highest thought of existence, that has been formed by Him, and by His re-creating Spirit, and according to the blood shed, that we are now to be trained to prove what is His perfect, and good, and acceptable will.

We have, in studying this subject in the connection in which it is thus given, to look at three thoughts especially—*the measure* of His will, *the rule* to guide us in following that will, and the *power* given for proving that will.

Let me draw attention to this, that it is not to prove the good, and perfect, and acceptable *work* of God; it is His *will*, not His *work*. It is not merely active service, such as evangelizing, or preaching the Gospel, or teaching, or in any way being ministers or evangelists, and so on. This is for the whole body of believers at every place where they may be. The lowest servant in the godless man's household, doing the most menial work, may have a high, a holy, and heavenly calm, and rest, and joy, and satisfaction, in doing his daily work, and doing it as to the Lord, feeling that he was proving that good, and holy, and acceptable will of God, and that in the place that God had put him, and with the work that God had given him. He ought not to rush away, and perhaps get into work whereto he was not sent, but calmly—not only at an occasional time, as on Sunday, when he could do a little tract-distributing, or something else—but, moment by moment, on Monday and Tuesday, every day, and every hour of every day, calmly be doing everything, with the consciousness within him that he and the Lord were in the same school—the Lord as the Master, and he as the willing scholar, being taught " the good, the perfect, and the acceptable will of God."

Nothing short of this is God's ideal for us. " Lo, I come to do Thy will. In the volume of the Book it is written of Me. I delight to do Thy will, O Lord !" And when He came here, Satan's first temptation was to make Him go out of that path; for he said, " If Thou be the Son of God." From the moment Christ came to do His Father's will, He had no will of His own. He went about doing many mighty deeds, because God was with Him. He took the place of a perfect man, a man in subjection to the will of another ; and thus showed His Godhead. Those who deny the Godhead of Christ point to Christ's own words—"My Father is greater than I." Why it is the very proof of His equality.

Take a human illustration. If two partners, equal in business, had a great number of servants, and they found that they were not obeyed, and one of the partners said, " Now we must teach them a lesson in obedience, and in not having their own wills. And so I will go and do your will." He asks no questions when the command is given, for whatever it may be given. If the other partner comes in and says, " You go and do such a menial work," the partner goes away, to the astonishment of the servants, and they say, "Why, you are equal in partnership; why go and do this menial work ?" "I am a servant in the meantime," he replies, "and the master is greater than the servant."

Thus Christ took the servant's place so thoroughly, that at every moment He acted from this motive, " Lo, I come to do Thy will," and will do so until the kingdom being delivered to God the Father, God is *all* in *all*. He is not now doing His own will ; He is set down on His Father's throne. He took the cup from His Father's hand, and will take the crown also. It is not given the Son of Man to know the times, but God Himself will give the crown to Him, and He will wait the Lord's time.

If we take this thought in reading the Gospel, that there was a perfect servant doing the acceptable will of God, many of these texts will explain themselves. He will wait the time that the Father takes to give Him His own throne ; for " He must reign until He hath put down all authority, and then shall the Son deliver up the kingdom to God the Father, that God may be all in all"—in that eternal day that is to dawn.

The measure, then, is the perfection of Christ. It is not mere law ; it is not " thou shalt " or " thou shalt not "—which brought out the inability of man, as sprung from Adam, to rise up to the level of human righteousness—but it is the grace of God in all He was, in all He said, in all He did ; this is the measure that we are called upon to follow.

We find His will revealed in the written Word, as we find His example in the Incarnate Word. We have in the written Word, the will of the Lord revealed to us so far as concerns our path here—that will which, by and by, will perfect us by making us subject to it ; that blessed will that, as it were, turns back the whole of a man's being, and gives it back to God again in the perfection that God Himself has provided—not merely the imputed righteousness or justifying of a man, but a man made morally like God, morally like the Christ of God, and moulded and fashioned to manifest to the angels, and the principalities, and the powers, through the ages to come, the wonders that God has wrought, the exceeding riches of His grace, the wonders of His righteousness, the manifestation of infinite holiness and infinite grace, and the bond that unites them—His infinite wisdom. This is the purpose for which we have been called of God, justified by God, are being sanctified, and soon will be glorified and made perfect with Him. What a glorious destiny !

What a fearful thing, then, self-will is—that will of Adam

that "brought death into the world, with all its woe!" Self-will and sin are just interchangeable terms. What is sin? Self-will. And what is self-will? Sin. Self is man's centre. Round him must revolve all in heaven and earth, it matters not how tiny or minute the little self. Even the less the self, the mightier the thoughts of the importance of all falling down before it. Self is man's centre. By faith we have changed our centre; we have got into the true astronomy of the heavens. We have found Christ, the centre; for everything in heaven and earth, and, I may say, under the earth, in hell (for all is linked and related to Him) revolve round Him. We have taken our stand upon Him, and rejoice in Him; and as we study our Bibles, from Christ the centre, and as we live our lives from Christ the centre, and as we mould our conduct from Christ the centre, so shall all our study, and all our thoughts, all our ways, and all our words, manifest the true harmony of the heavens of God, and send up in all our actions a constant psalm of praise. By Him we shall be offering "the sacrifice of praise continually—that is the fruit of our lips giving thanks to His name." The old philosophers dreamed of the stars singing round the throne of God, but here will be true worship in the moulding of our hearts to Him, proving the good, the perfect, and the acceptable will of God.

The power is given to take that Word, and not merely have it in our heads, and know the doctrines clearly and exactly. It is not the mere pages of the Word that are of value to us; it is not the mere printing, or the doctrine contained in it. It is, as that written Word forms the Incarnate Word within us, and the Incarnate Word goes out in activity in doing the will of God that the Spirit takes of the things of Christ, and makes us drink into the river of His own good pleasure. Thus we get the Holy Spirit sent to indwell within us, to prove the good, and holy, and acceptable will of God, going onward in the path of Him who said, "Take My yoke upon you, and learn of Me; for I am meek and lowly in heart, and ye shall find rest to your souls."

It is not merely "Come unto Me, and I will give you rest." That is to the unsaved sinner. There is nothing between the unsaved sinner, and the seeking Saviour but the man's unbelief. When sinners are brought to God, there is salvation; but there is a yoke put on after the coming to Christ—"Take My yoke

upon you." This is for those who have accepted the Gospel.
What was the yoke of Christ? If you remember, in the
eleventh chapter of Matthew, it says that He had been doing
most of His mighty deeds in certain cities of the land of
Canaan, and the cities wherein He had done most of His
mighty deeds would not have Him; and then He pronounced
His woes upon them in judgment. "Woe unto thee, Chorazin!
woe unto thee, Bethsaida!" There was the yoke—doing good
and being cast out. We ourselves do not like to do good, and
to be cast out. Doing good, and being ill-used for doing it;
doing good to all men, having a heart of love to every man,
to the poorest and most wretched upon earth—to do good to
those, and to be cast out, is a yoke hard to bear. Well, in
those cities Christ did most of His mighty deeds; and as they
cast Him out, He had to pronounce His woes upon them, and
that was His yoke. It is human nature for us to wish people
to like what we say and teach, and to be patted on the back for
it, and to be "appreciated," as it is called; that is not the
yoke. You find it in Peter. "To do good, and suffer for it,
and take it patiently;" that is grace. This is the more exact
translation of it: "To do good, and suffer for it, and take it
patiently"—a very hard thing to do, and nothing but the grace
of God will enable us to do it. To do evil, and suffer for it,
and take it patiently, is only what we ought to do; but to do
good, and suffer for it, and take it patiently, that is grace in the
sight of God.

"Take My yoke upon you, and learn of Me, and ye shall
find rest." Where did He find His rest? The moment He
denounced Chorazin and Bethsaida, He turned to His Father
and raised His eyes to Heaven, but He does not say, "Lo this
world has rejected Me. I will go back to Thy bosom, and be
in that unspeakable calm as Thy Eternal Son." No, but He
turns His eyes to Heaven, and says, "I thank thee, O Father!"
—thanksgiving in the midst of abuse, thanksgiving with eyes
upturned to an open Heaven, and these revilers, and abusers,
and Pharisees, and Scribes, all about Him, like the bulls of
Bashan, ready to devour Him. "I thank Thee, O Father, Lord
of Heaven and earth." It says in Luke that He "rejoiced in
spirit." "I thank Thee, O Father, that Thou hast hid these
things from the wise and prudent, and hast revealed them unto
babes; even so, Father, for so it seemed good in Thy sight."

"Learn of Me for I am meek." How unlike what we are! "and lowly," going down under everything. Is that like us? "Stand up for your rights!" ah! that is old Adam, and we, that have been taken from old Adam into the new, know something better than speaking about our rights. We know perfectly well, when we are on this ground, that if it is standing up for our rights, we mean that we should have been all in the lake of fire for ever. Nothing short of that. That is our due.

And now we are to be meek and lowly, not merely in the external appearance (that can be put on), but meek and lowly in heart. Are we prepared to follow Him? Are we prepared to learn of Him? Are we prepared to go in the paths of Him who said, "I come to do Thy will"? Count the cost. It is hard self-denial, the breaking of the human will, and the moulding of that will into the will of God. All the principles of the old Adam are entirely swept away, and "Learn of Me" can stand in the midst of the fire of the artillery of man's wrath as calm as the God of Heaven's calmness can make it.

What a calm man a Spirit-filled man should be—calm amidst the wreck of worlds, the ruin of empires, and the great crash of the world's catastrophe at last; still calm you "shall find rest," and the more yoke-bearing, the more rest-finding. That is, the more that we learn of Him, the more we are merged into His will, and prove it. "If any man will serve Me, let Him follow Me." I think we sometimes read it the other way—"If any man will follow Me, he must serve Me." That is not how it reads in the 12th of John, "If any man will serve Me, let him follow Me." There is no such Christless service. All that we are to do for Him let it be with a single eye, and while we ask, " Is this *what* He would have me do? *how* He would have me do it? and *when* He would have me to do it? and the *spirit in which* He would have me to do it, if He had been here?" Let us remember His words, "If any man will serve Me, let him follow Me."

And we have all the provision given us by the blessed Spirit. The Spirit has given us to know our need, in order that we may take up the yoke, and go and find rest, and prove His will here. We will have it in perfection by and by.

The Lord Himself, knowing our weakness, and knowing the condition of His disciples, taught them to pray in those their circumstances, that inimitable prayer that we all know so well, but that we ofttimes think so little about. In that prayer, commonly called "the Lord's prayer," but more correctly the disciples' prayer (the Lord's prayer being John xvii), we have every provision in every condition, from the highest, and always descending to the lowest, in doing His will. We have to pray, "Thy will be done on earth as it is in Heaven." And we have before this, "Our Father, which art in Heaven." There is the highest relationship of all, the *sons of the Father*, and, as children, being far from home, in fact, but made nigh by faith, we can draw near unto Him. Next we come down a little, "Hallowed be Thy name." We are now *worshipers in the Temple*, reverently hallowing the name of the Lord—sons and worshipers. "Thy kingdom come." We are also *kings waiting for a kingdom*. Angels are worshipers, but they are not kings waiting for a kingdom, and we say, "Thy kingdom come," in which we are to reign with Him, as we suffer with Him now. But if sons, and worshipers, and kings, we are also *servants aiming at perfect obedience*, and we say, "Thy will be done on earth as it is in heaven." But if we are sons and worshipers, and kings, and servants, we are also *needy dependents* and we say, "Give us this day our daily bread," all our needs always anticipated, and always met with the most perfect wisdom. But we are lower than needy dependents; we are *sinners requiring forgiveness*. "Forgive us our debts, as we forgive our debtors." Grace saves us forever, but His government regulates our lives here according to His laws. But more than that, we are not only sinners, but *sinners ready to be led astray*. "Lead us not into temptation." And, further than that, to the very lowest depths of all, we have a great enemy going about seeking whom he may devour, his net round about us trying to entrap us—the wicked one. Hence, "But deliver us from the wicked one;" for such is the full force of the word used. It is not merely indefinite evil, but a person—"deliver us from the wicked one"—whose existence is being so sadly denied in these days; and thus his own tactics are being carried out. God preserve us from this! From sons of the Father, down to those that have to meet the wiles of the devil in performing the will of God, all is anticipated by the blessed Spirit of God, and all has been met in the provision of His grace, as sons, worshipers, kings, servants, dependents, sinners, tempted ones, besieged ones. We know that path, wherein we prove the good, and acceptable, and perfect will of God the path which no fowl knoweth, and which the vulture's eye has never seen, and the lion's whelps have not trodden it, nor the fierce lion passed by it.   And may it be to us day by day as in the language of the beautiful hymn—

> " I bow me to Thy will, O God,
>   And all Thy paths adore ;
> And every day I live I'll seek
>   To serve Thee more and more.
>
> When obstacles and trials seem
>   Like prison-walls to be ;
> I do the little I can do,
>   And leave the rest to Thee.
>
> And when it seems no chance or change
>   From grief can set me free,
> Hope finds its strength in helplessness,
>   And patient, waits on Thee.
>
> Man's weakness, waiting upon God,
>   Its end can never miss ;
> For men on earth no work can do
>   More angel-like than this.
>
> Lead on, lead on triumphantly,
>   O blessed Lord, lead on !
> Faith's pilgrim sons behind Thee seek
>   The path that Thou hast gone.
>
> He always wins who sides with God,
>   To him no chance is lost ;
> God's will is sweetest to him when
>   It triumphs at his cost."

WALKING WITH GOD.

"*And Enoch walked with God; and he was not; for God took him.*"—GENESIS V. 24.

"*Noah was a just man,* * * * *and walked with God.*"—GENESIS vi. 9.

WALKING WITH GOD.

PETER walked with God, and he was enabled to walk in a very wonderful place, because he walked upon the word of God. "If it be Thou, Lord, bid me come to Thee." And Jesus said, "Come;" and on that word,—Peter walked upon the sea, for the word of God is much stronger than the law of gravitation, or any other law. When God speaks, the sea is His, and it obeys Him. Then Peter began to sink, and he found that the sea was not so solid after all. And why? Because he looked upon the boisterous waves; and, in fact, the boisterous waves had nothing to do with the matter, because it was as easy to walk over the boisterous waves as over a smooth sea. But, you see, unbelief is always foolish. Faith is always wise. But faith does not contradict reason, it transcends it, it rises above it. I can reason that I am specifically heavier than water; but when God tells me to come over the water, specific laws, and specific gravity, and everything else, have to obey the Lawgiver; and thus I quite object to the controversy that there is between true science and revelation. I love science. We all love true science, when science can teach us. But science cannot tell me how to walk with God.

Then there are other saints that have been in strange places walking with God. There were three dear ones away in the olden time that, instead of walking on water, were walking through fire. And why? Because God was with them, and "one like unto the Son of God" was there, and there was no burning. They did not know but that they might be burnt, for they said, "Our God is able to deliver us from the burning fiery furnace, but if not"—oh! I love the faith which is in that "if not." I think there is more faith often in the "if not" than in saying, "We can be protected." Any man could go in and say "I may be protected." But they said, "But if not, we will not worship your image. We will be faithful to God in spite of fire or anything else." But they went into the fire, and nothing was burnt, as we all well know. They were thrown in bound, but they were seen walking with God.

Another wondrous march with God—another wonderful walk —one of the most wonderful walks I know of in all history— "It came to pass after these things that God did tempt Abraham, and said unto him, Abraham," and the ear was open. It was no itching ear. It was an open ear, and he said, "Here am I." The itching ear listens to man. Some people buy the new Revised Testament and that they think that they have got a new Bible. They say that it is something easier than our old-fashioned evangelistic Bible. Thank God, everything stands as it was as far as all the essentials are concerned. They want something new. But Abraham was wont to listen to his God, and he said, "Here am I." And God said, "Take now thy son." Oh, what a trial! "The son of thy old age"—the son of faith—the son of resurrection-power! "Take now thy son." And God dilates upon it, as if to intensify it. "Thine only son." Not only so, but He names him, "Isaac"—not Ishmael. "Thine only son Isaac." He adds to it still—"Whom thou lovest." What intensity of trial! "That the trial of your faith might be as gold that is tried in the fire." "Take now thy son, thine only son Isaac, whom thou lovest, and get thee into the land of Moriah; and offer him there for a burnt-offering upon one of the mountains that I will tell thee of." What is the result? "Abraham rose up early in the morning." He might have been permitted to sleep on till midday with such a journey before him. But prompt is his obedience. "Early in the morning," as if anxious to obey, even to cut his own heart-strings, "early in the morning, and saddled his ass, and took two of his young men with him, and Isaac his son, and clave the wood for the burnt-offering, and rose up, and went unto the place of which God had told him." Then "on the third day"—think of that— three days' walk with God—three days to think over it—three days to get to Mount Moriah. It seems to me much harder than Peter's attempt and failure—much harder than the three Hebrew children's attempt and success—this protracted thinking and revolving, with his loved son at his side, walking onward, and onward only, upon the word of the everlasting God, day succeeding night, and night succeeding day, and his own heart breaking, and his heart going up to God. And he said, " Did I hear God ? Do I know God ? Have I His word under me?" "Take thy son, thine only son Isaac, whom thou lovest, and offer him."

At the end of a very spiritual and delightful meeting, when our hearts are filled with love to our Master and His truth, if an enemy should come and seize us, and say, "Now we must take your life, or you must bow down and worship an image." I believe that a great number of us in the heat and warmth of our spiritual life would be prepared to say, "Take my life, then, and have done with it." That would be in the heat of the moment. We could do lots of things in the heat of the moment, when we are warmed up, which we could not do in what is called cold blood. But there was no heat of the moment here in this walking with God, but persistent, steady, strong faith, and there was everything against him. If you had gone to Abraham then, and said, " Abraham how do you feel as a father? What is your paternal affection like ?" he would have said, " Do not speak to me ;" and he would wipe the tear from his eye. " What do you think of a man going to kill a fellow-man ?" " Do not speak to me." Abraham believed God. That was all. " And how do you feel to God, Abraham ? That is the son that the promise is given to, and the coming seed is to spring from him. God's name will be dishonoured, and God's cause and God's purposes will be foiled." "God can look after His own purposes ; I have only to obey." What a sight ! Oh, if we had but the power of some great painter to picture that wondrous scene under that eastern sky ! The faith of Isaac, too, must have been strong. Remember that he was not a young lad. He was a strong, stalwart young man, in his prime, and to allow himself to be bound and laid upon the altar to be an offering to God was a part of his faith got from his father's teaching, and there, as the young man lay, every bit of Abraham's heart goes against the act which he has to do. In Abraham's heart his parental love, his human feelings, and his regard for God's purposes are all against it. There is a calm, silent sky above him, and the mountain beside him and beneath him, and he lifts up the dagger with that hand ; and he has nothing to support him but the word of God. There is nothing between him and God, but God's word, "The mouth of the Lord has spoken it," and the knife comes down, and it falls upon the arm of Jehovah. God is never too late. The angel said, "There is a ram." The angel comes and says, "Stay thy hand." He lifted up his eyes to look, and beheld the substitute. Oh, friends, it may be on the water, it may be through the fire, it may be through the bitterest trial, but it is the God that is in it that makes the walk glorious.

My heart has been thinking to-day of the God that we have to walk with—not so much the walk, but the *God* that we have to walk with. We have a glorious aspect of the truth in walking, as showing companionship. It does; but it also shows identification. I would not like every man to come and take me by the arm, and walk with me down the streets—not likely! I am identified with his character to that extent. The man whose arm I take, and I are quite content to change characters, one with the other, to a certain extent, as far as it can be done. But here we are the representatives of God upon this earth, to let the world know about God; and our walking with God is to show the people what God is like. Alas! alas! how the Church has failed!

I remember a statement that I heard not many years ago from one who has the best right of any man living to give an opinion upon it, and that was Lord Shaftesbury. As he stood at a meeting, and as I sat by his side, he said these awful words—true and awful, because true—"that he had been identified with a great number of humanizing influences and activities during the last half-century, and he had seen humanity improved, and classes being drawn together; but the more that he saw them getting improved in that way, the further they were getting from God." I would not have dared to make that statement myself, because I have not the practical information; but from lips such as those of that honored man of God, and that honored philanthropist, I think they are most weighty words for us to ponder, and which should make us ask ourselves why it is that God is being shown out of His world, and why we are not walking to manifest Him.

God is the great fact that the world needs—a living God for a dead world. The speaking from the divine into the human —from heaven to earth—from the eternal into time—is the whole history of these six millenniums—the whole history of

the Bible from Genesis to Revelation.   From the creation of
the world to the great white throne, and beyond it, God is the
idea.   What does a man that does not want God, see upon
opening the Bible?   "In the beginning God created——"
The fourth word is "God," and the first chapter has five-and-
thirty mentions of the one solemn word, "God"—God the
Creator and the Ruler, making all, forming all, none to help
Him, none to hinder Him.   Go down to the last point in history, beyond the new heavens and the new earth, in Rev. xxi.,
and further on in the eternal day you will find again the word
comes up.   Six times there, we read the word "God," when
Christ has delivered up the kingdom to His Father, that
God may be all in all.   And we are men of God, and men
walking with God, and men working for God; and this is our
position, and the reason of our existence here—that men may
know of God.

And, above all, the typical man that we have, whose history
has been before us, is the grand old preacher, the first
of all preachers that we read of—Enoch.   We have his
walk in Genesis.   We have the foundation of that walk in
Hebrews.   We have the outcome of that walk in Jude.   And
we have a threefold history of the great man—walking with God
in the midst of times very like our own; for if you look at his
testimony, you will find in Jude, that "Enoch, the seventh from
Adam, prophesied of these things to those round about him,
saying, Behold, the Lord cometh with the myriads of His saints,
to execute judgment upon all, and to convince all that are ungodly among them, of all their ungodly deeds which they have
ungodly committed, and of all their hard speeches which ungodly sinners have spoken against Him."   Four times the word
"ungodly" is in that one chapter, and four times does this
man of God, who walked by faith with God, on God's word,
throw it in the teeth of these men that there is a God, and that
there is a judgment, and that God is coming in judgment, and
the thing that will be judged is their ungodliness, and their
want of knowing God—"the ungodly deeds which they have
committed, and all their hard speeches which ungodly sinners
have spoken against Him."   It is not that we care for ourselves.
It is what they have said against God, "enduring such contradiction of sinners against Himself."   And it is a remarkable
thing, that when we have come in Hebrews to find how it was

that Enoch walked with God, we find that by faith Enoch was translated, that he should not see death. By faith he walked, and by faith he was translated; and it is added in Hebrews, that he was not found. And why? He believed that God was the Rewarder of them that diligently seek Him. He diligently sought God, and therefore found God; and when he found God, the world could not find him. And so it is, we shall be sure to be utterly unable to be made out by the world if we have found God. They cannot make us out if we walk with God. The walk with God is of such a character that the world knows nothing about it. They cannot find us. Translated or not translated, we are utterly unfindable by them.

There is a similar statement in the second chapter of the book of Kings, of another mysterious disappearing one. When Elijah was caught up similarly to Enoch, we find that Elisha came and told it; but they said to him, " Behold, now there be with thy servant fifty strong men, the sons of the prophets" (fifty theological students.) " Let them go, we pray thee, and seek the master." There was rationalism, you see, in colleges then; they will not believe a word that Elisha says about God having taken Elijah, and so they appointed a rationalistic committee. " Let them go, we pray thee, and seek thy master lest peradventure "—here is the reason: they could not believe that he was gone, that he had walked with God, and that he was caught up with God to walk with Him for ever—"lest peradventure "—man is always coming in with his " lest peradventures "—"lest peradventure the Spirit of the Lord hath taken him up, and cast him upon some mountain" thown him back again—"cast him upon some mountain or into some valley," as if the Holy Ghost made such mistakes that He could not end the journey if he had begun it. They believed not in Him. " He cannot begin it, He cannot uphold us, He cannot preserve, He cannot keep us when He has got us." That was the rationalistic reasoning of this committee of theological students. " And he said, Ye shall not send." Well done, Professor Elisha ! That was well done for the teacher; he said, "Ye shall not send." He stood upon the word of God. But they urged him till he was ashamed—"a little leaven leavens the whole lump "—and he said, " Send." He came down after all.

When we see Elisha coming down and being influenced thus, the Lord preserve us all from that which is so truly sad, and

which is sapping the very morality, and the very life of the
Church of God. When we see what is being taught in high
quarters we may all well tremble, and look out for our sons of
the prophets, and look out for our Elishas, and go to the living
God, and walk with Him in truth. We will neither have the
Romanism on the one side, which tells us of a cross without a
Christ, nor the rationalism on the other side, which tells us of a
Christ without a cross. We are "determined to know nothing
among men save Jesus Christ and Him crucified." When God
was about to walk here below, what was said of Him? "He
shall be called Emmanuel"—"God with us." He came—He
does not say, "I come simply as God to be your example, or
your friend, or to lead you, or to be your teacher." "She shall
bring forth a Son, and they shall call His name Jesus; for He
shall save His people from their sins." "And all this was done
that it might be fulfilled which was written, Behold, a virgin
shall bring forth a Son, and they shall call his name Emmanuel." People might say, "He is not called Emmanuel."
Friend, you are not taking the New Testament commentary,
written by the Holy Ghost, on the Old Testament truth. The
Old Testament truth was "Emmanuel." God is to be with
us. But look at the tremendous truth involved in that—God
cannot visit this world as a friend, as a teacher, as a leader, as
a rationalistic great one. If He is to come at all, He must come
as Jesus, the Saviour, to save His people from their sins; and
if a Saviour is to be provided for sinners, nothing but "Emmanuel" can be the Saviour—nothing but "God with us." If all
the angels, and seraphs, and cherubs, and created intelligences
that ever were created by God had been executed in man's
behalf, not a single sinner could have got to glory; for after
they had given back their lives, they had only received their
lives from God, and they were bound to give Him all that He
had given before. It was only the uncreated One that was for
ever in the bosom of the Father, "God manifest in the flesh,"
that could become our "Jesus to save His people from
their sins."

I must close with the testimony that Enoch, this great
teacher from God, gave us. He walked with God. It is
one of the most difficult lessons which I have to learn, to go
into my closet and shut the door, and there talk with
God, realizing first that God is; and secondly, that He is a

Rewarder of them that diligently seek Him. Enoch came to Him. He walked with Him; he pleased Him. And mark how pleasing is put in connection with walking, as in Col. i. 10: "That ye might walk worthy of the Lord unto all pleasing." And Enoch before his translation received the testimony that he "pleased God." He was taken to Him, he was translated by Him; he is with Him; and he will return again with Him, when the rest of us come back as the Master comes to fulfil in all its fulness that great prophecy which Enoch, the seventh from Adam, was privileged to give. Enoch, one who walked with God, walking on His word, walking by His word, walking through His word, and God filling all—God filling my theology, God filling my family, God filling my life, God filling my testimony. Some who will not go to the extreme length of rationalism have tried to get as little of God in the Bible as they can. We want as much of God as we can get hold of in all Scripture—a Scripture full of God from its beginning to its end, our testimony full of God, our life full of God: "For to me to live is Christ."—To "WALK WITH GOD."

Now, friends, let us be practical as we close this subject. Just let us take a slip of paper, and do not write that text which I have begun to quote, but let us be upright before God. There is the walking which the psalmist speaks of—"No good thing will He withhold from them that walk uprightly." We need a great deal of practical uprightness, uprightness of soul with God; not playing with religion; not trafficking with truth; but straight up and down with God—honour bright before Him, and honour bright with our fellow-men, walking uprightly there. Let us be conscientious and not slip it over, veneering it before God. It is to live we want. The word in Hebrew which says that "Enoch walked with God," means that Enoch walked *habitually* with God. It was the habit, the tendency, the bent of the whole man. Let us go away, preachers and hearers, and say, "For to me to live is——," then fill in the blank for yourself. I cannot fill it for you. By grace I try to fill it in for myself. I am speaking of Christians, remember. We know what Paul said: "For to me to live is"—pleasure? enjoyment? meetings? religious service? visiting the sick? Sometimes the more holy the things are, the worse they may become. "For to me to live——." I know some genuine Christians whom I have met, and I fear that there are many more, who invert the text, and they think that Christ is a nice pillow to lie upon on a death-bed, and then when they get to glory it will be so happy to see Him ; and their work seems to be this: "For me to live is gain, and to die will be Christ." If we had a little less of that, you would not have to be pleading for monies to carry on Missions. This would not be so if gain were less before the minds even of Christian people, and they knew that it sanctified gain to give it to Him who has given all for us; for, though we may speak ofttimes very happily about it, it cost Him everything. He loved us and gave Himself for us, and if we can fill it in with the Apostle in some degree, "For to me to live is *Christ,*" it may seem a rough way, and it may seem a thorny way, but—

> " There is but that path in the waste
>   Which His footsteps have marked as His own,
> And I follow in diligent haste
>   To the seats where He's put on His crown."

It *is* thorny. We do not believe in the broad way, we do not believe in the delightful way ; but we believe in the true way —the true, and the new, and the living way, and the path that may seem rough ; for we believe that—

> "'Tis first the true, and then the beautiful,
>   Not first the beautiful, and then the true ;
> First the wild moor, with rock, and reed, and pool,
>   Then the gay garden, rich in scent and hue.

> "'Tis first the good, and then the beautiful,
>   Not first the beautiful, and then the good ;
> First the rough seed, sown in the rougher soil,
>   Then the flower-blossom, on the branching wood.

> " Not first the glad, and then the sorrowful,
>   But first the sorrowful, and then the glad ;
> Tears for a day, for earth of tears is full,
>   Then we forget that we were ever sad.

> " Not first the bright, and after that the dark,
>   But first the dark, and after that the bright ;
> First the thick cloud, and then the rainbow's arc,
>   First the dark grave, then resurrection light.

> " 'Tis first the night—stern night of storm and war—
>   Long night of heavy clouds and veiled skies ;
> Then the fair sparkle of the Morning Star,
>   That bids the saints awake, and dawn arise."

CHRISTIAN WARFARE.

" *Wherefore take unto you the whole armour of God, that ye may be able to withstand in the evil day, and having done all, to stand. Stand therefore, having your loins girt about with truth, and having on the breastplate of righteousness: and your feet shod with the preparation of the gospel of peace; above all, taking the shield of faith, wherewith ye shall be able to quench all the fiery darts of the wicked. And take the helmet of salvation, and the sword of the Spirit, which is the word of God.*"—EPHESIANS vi. 13-17.

CHRISTIAN WARFARE.

OUR strength is in a knowledge and confession of weakness, and the realization of an unseen, but real God. Before we can hope to fight successfully, we must become supplicants and dependents. Prayer is not offered with a view to change God's plans, but to show that we are dependent and confident. It is part of the design of God that we, worms of the dust, should hang upon, and trust in Him. It was not the worm Jacob that was to thresh the mountains, but he prevailed with the angel when his thigh was out of joint—in his weakness. As long as we have energy in the flesh to wrestle, we have not the dependence of the worm to hang, trust, and cling to the feet of the Angel of the Covenant, saying, " I will not let Thee go unless Thou bless me."

QUALIFICATION.

In 1 John ii., middle of the 14th verse, we read, " I have written unto you, young men, because ye are strong." The speciality of young men is that they are strong, and they glory in their strength. That strength to be used to bring about the end for which it is intended, requires to have, in the first place, *a living man* to wield it, and we must have the constitution that can fight. We " must be born again," for we have not a single power within us by nature. God does not find us soldiers, sons, nor heirs, but makes us such. And now that He has begotten us into His family, are we not a kingdom of priests to Him? Are we not His soldiers now, to use His strength and armour, and to exercise our arm in the use of His sword, "the sword of the Spirit, which is the word of God."

CONDITIONS OF SERVICE.

Having thus seen wherein our strength consists there is the word, "If any man will come after me, let him deny himself." Not merely abstain from luxuries or comforts. We have a deeper thought in the sentence. The first thing is to deny *myself*—my existence altogether as a man. Paul challenged some that they lived as men. We are not to live as *mere* men, but as sons of God. What do I confess? Christ alone. I live, walk, speak Christ. "For to me to live *is* Christ," not self. I deny my own power to save myself, to live to God, or to move a finger. The next thought we take up—" I have written unto you, young men . . . the word of God abideth in you." There is the secret of strength.

There is no man strong from the divine standpoint, but the man in whom His word abides. You may have all the intelligence of past ages gathered up into one brain, and may be a very Plato, Socrates, or Shakespeare, but if you have not the Word of God in you, He does not allow the word "strong" to be applied to you.

This is the great characteristic of the Lord's warriors, of that class of soldiers that come to the front ; and John evidently puts them in the fore-front of the battle as the young men of valor, strength, and activity. I believe, dear friends, that as we go onward towards the latter days, more and more will this Word of God be the rallying point for the Lord's own. We get tired of sectional fightings in the Church of God ; we get sick of men reasoning about their "isms." We respect every man's ecclesiastical convictions, and ignore no man's ; to his own Master he stands or falls ; but there is a higher level than each man looking out for his corner of the garden, where he thinks, perhaps, the truth of God may be best seen. I would like to have the blessing of Joseph. He was a fruitful bough, and his branches ran over the wall. Rejoice to be able to run over the walls of all the denominations.

THE PRESENT WARFARE.

The battle at the present day is about the Word of God. Ignorant and learned alike are attacking it. It is the key to the position, as a certain farm was at Waterloo. The enemy are trying to turn our flank ; for you find but few advocates of the coarse atheism of former days. Perhaps some vulgar fluent speakers may try to catch people by speaking strongly about no God ; but there is no great thinking unbeliever of the present day who has the madness to deny God's existence. They acknowledge Him under various names ; and in the recent work of that sadly wonderful man, John Stuart Mill, he takes the position that if any man succeeds in believing that there is a God—wonderful experiment, you know !—we can never prove the proposition to be untrue. That is a great admission from a professed unbeliever. In fact it is only a *fool* who can say there is no God. Unphilosophical, unscientific, irrational—"The fool has said in his heart, there is no God."

THE ENEMY'S POSITION.

A man may say he has lived here, and never saw any marks of God. Well, if you spent a summer in the moon, you might find that there is One who would overcome even your scepticism. Man must search every corner of the universe before he can say there is no God. And not only so ; he must be in every star at the same time, for if he left one for another, he might be a moment too late. If I have to say there is no arsenic in this glass of water, how many tests must I not employ ? At my examination in chemistry, the question, "What is pure water ?" nearly overthrew me. The unbeliever asks you to believe that he himself is God.

Can God speak ? If you say no, you reach the absurdity that He who made the mouth cannot speak. The third question is, Has He spoken ? If you say no, you land yourself in the dilemma of having an immoral God, one who could let you know what He required, and would not. We must answer, He has spoken. What has He said ? "I have written to you, young men, because the word of God abideth in you." How do I know it? I will tell you the best test. "Come, see a man that told me all that ever I did." Come, see a book that tells me all that ever I did, and alone satisfies my conscience with a righteous God, and yet a God of love. Is not that the divine book ? You may know it, as you know the sun shines, —by opening your eyes.

If a man came and told me to strike a match in order to see

the new light he had invented, I should say, "Well, if the light cannot show itself, there is none. But the reason people have doubts about the Book is because they do not get it in the right line. They try to get it through the head instead of the conscience. The revelation *must* come through that which puts the man before God in his true moral light.

GOD'S GREAT ONES.

The greatest revelations ever made to mankind were not to great philosophers, reasoners, and thinkers ; none such clustered round Christ. "I that spake unto thee am He," was addressed to a poor self-confessed sinner. To whom did He make the revelation, "I ascend to my Father and your Father"? To the two great theologians, Peter and John? No : they ran away too soon. But to a poor weeping woman, whose conscience was thoroughly at one with her God, and whose heart was longing for her Lord. This poor woman heard the accents, "Mary," and knew her Lord. Ah ! the microscopic revelations of those tears. I have never been able to convince any by argument of the truth of anything got from the Bible. It is like David putting on Saul's armour.

OUR WEAPON.

If you run a sword through a man's body you have not to prove it is a sword. So use the Word. Some tell me the Bible is not the Word of God ; but let us prove it by a simple illustration. If I have a book enabling me to put all the parts of a sewing-machine together, I know the writer is a maker of that machine. We are as poor machines out of order, but by looking into the word our spirits are corrected. Pilate, like an owl shutting its eyes, asks, "What is Truth?" Did not Christ say, "I am the Truth." The youngest man who has accepted God's revelation may say, "I know the Truth." I am wanting to know more of truth ; but I am not ignorant as to where to find it.

What a glorious thing to have a firm tread, and not like man with his wisdom, trying to find the stars among the sands of the sea-shore, or to build a tower up to heaven. We know the incarnate Word, Jesus, who has given us this written word. We have certainty ; our responsibility is now to let it abide,— live with us. The word made you a child of God. "By His own will begat He us, by the word of truth." "Faith cometh by hearing, and hearing by the word of God." I used to pray, cry, and open my mouth wide for faith ; but it is now, I will *hear* what God the Lord will speak." "Hear, and your souls shall live." God speaks: I will listen.

But Christian life is a continual warfare. It is easy enough to think lightly of sin ; but the more light in a house the better we see. I see the evil of my heart now, more than when I came to Christ at first. We have to fight all the way along, for we find we are prone to sin.

Now, by what means "shall a young man cleanse his way? By taking heed thereto according to Thy Word." What a beautiful figure is the "water" of the Word. See Ephesians v. 26, and John iii. Look at the action of water in cleansing ; your ideas and mine are as foul mud, and the first thing you need is to be washed out of all your thoughts by the Word.

It is still a hard fight which the Christian carries on throughout his course ; if you are full of God's thoughts you will have no room for the devil's. The "word is a lamp to our feet," and we only know it as the darkness comes around us. Here is a man who takes, to light him on a windy night, a lucifer match; but out it goes. See the man with the strong, steady light of God's Word. When Satan comes to you, do not try him with your experience as is often done, but give him a text. You do not become swordsmen in a day, remember. Some come to me and say, "Does it not say so and so somewhere in the Bible." My friend, you have hold of the sword by the wrong end. We want young men in whom the Word abides to treasure the word in your breast. Wield the sword of the Spirit, and you will have constant victory.

THE CHRISTIAN LIVING ON EARTH.

" *Now, the just shall live by faith.*"—HEBREWS X. 38.

" *For to me to live is Christ, and to die is gain.*"—PHILIPPIANS i. 21.

THE CHRISTIAN LIVING ON EARTH.

OUR subject is:—"The Christian living on earth." Not
the mere moralist, but the Christian. The Christian, not
in heaven, but the Christian living on earth. The subject before us is not a fancy; is not a feeling; is not a doctrine.
It is what it is stated to be—a Christian living.

The Christian is "to live;" not merely to be saved, and to
praise Christ's name together in happy joy ; nor to acknowledge
Him in all His perfections as a man, but to manifest His life
upon the earth.

I wish now to briefly draw your attention to this fact : that
no fancy, however high, no feeling however deep, and no doctrine, however sound, can make up Christian living. Christian
living must be originated in heaven, in the life of God Himself ;
Christian living must come down from heaven to earth, in the
presence of Him who said to us, "I am the Way, the Truth, and
the Life," and Christian living must be communicated by Him
who has been sent from the Father and the Son—the Third
Person of the glorious Trinity, to beget that great reality within
us, and to make us sons and daughters of the Lord God Almighty—begotten of God.

In the first place, I draw your attention to a passage in God's
Word that shows us the common tenure of this life in the saints
of all ages. For I believe that no sinner was saved or shall be
saved, from the days of Abel down to the days of the great
white throne, but by being cleansed in the blood of Christ, and
regenerated by the Holy Ghost. I take you to an Old Testament prophet, perhaps little read in these days, Habakkuk.
The third chapter speaks of Habakkuk resigning himself to the
words of God, and falling under His rod in submission, if not

in joy. He finishes by telling us that even " though the fig-tree shall not blossom, neither shall fruit be in the vines ; the labour of the olive shall fail, and the fields shall yield no meat ; the flock shall be cut off from the fold, and there shall be no herd in the stalls, yet I will rejoice in the Lord ; I will joy in the God of my salvation. The Lord God is my strength, and He will make my feet like hinds' feet, and He will make me walk upon mine high places."

How is this consummation to be reached ?   In the first chapter of Habakkuk, where we find his burden, in the thirteenth verse, when he speaks to God, he says : " Thou canst not look on iniquity ; wherefore lookest Thou upon them that deal treacherously, and holdest Thy tongue when the wicked devoureth the man that is more righteous than he, and makest men as the fishes of the sea, as the creeping things, that have no ruler over them ?"   Are we not in a similar condition to-day ?   In the present day we see these things happening, and God silent amidst it all.   Falsehood and deceit, and murder and theft, and all that dishonors God, are seen all around, and He sits silent upon His throne of glory.   But "God shall come," says the Psalmist, "and shall not keep silence."   Habakkuk was waiting to be relieved of the burden that had pressed upon his soul, and ground him down ; he was waiting for the great and glorious emancipation that was to make him rise up to the throne of God, and be like Him, and with Him for ever.   This holy man waited for the revelation of God.   "Write it and make it plain upon tables of stone, that a man who reads it may run." Sometimes it is thought that the letters were to be so large and legible, that even a runner could read them ; but it really is that the reading of them may impart power to his running.   And thus we find in the Old Testament, the prophet Habakkuk receiving a special revelation from God, in the second chapter : "The just shall live by faith."   This beautiful text has been transfigured in glory by the apostle Paul, and three times we find in his writings this text used on various occasions : 1st, in the Epistle to the Romans ; 2nd, in the Epistle to the Galatians ; and 3rd, in the Epistle to the Hebrews.

This is Christian living; Christian living in its Alpha, Christian living in its omega, and Christian living all the way between.   Christian living to start with, Christian living to continue with, and Christian living to end with.   They first shall come into spiritual existence, into the living of Christ, into that love and fellowship with Christ by faith ; shall grow therein and be perfected therein.

I have had to do with many anxious inquirers, and I find the greatest stumbling-block of all is this: they wish to be able to feel faith. Even the telephone cannot let us *see* a sound ; it can let us *hear* a sound. You might as well speak of hearing a sight as feeling faith. "Faith is the substance of things hoped for; the evidence of things not seen." If feeling were justification, or were the means of applying justification, then this would be the consciousness of what was going on within. It is not faith in what is felt.

The just shall come into this relation of justified sons with God, by faith (Rom. i. 17),

"There is life in a look at the Crucified One."

All God's ways are unnatural, because we approach them by sense or feeling. All God's ways are against man's ideas. Moses, by divine command, had an extraordinary way of healing snake-bites. "You don't mean to tell me," any doctor would have said, "looking at this little bit of brass will stop that hemorrhage? Do you mean to say we have only to look to that brass?" It is not a question of what you have or feel. It was a revelation that came from a great God who had sent those serpents upon them. You must accept His thoughts and reject your own. He has revealed Himself. Sometimes men come to the Bible and think they can judge it. You can never judge a revelation of God. You can accept or reject it, but you cannot judge it. God's light shines upon every man in the world. It brings light, and life, and joy ; but a man that does not wish or require God, and does not wish for a revelation, must be left to find out that he does require those things. If our great theologians had to write that Bible of ours, it would have been a proper course to have begun by an introduction concerning the *a priori* or *a posteriori* argument for the existence of a God. But God makes no such preface. He says, "In the beginning God created." People are trying to make out the beginning of creation without a Creator ; they have been fighting all the days of thinking man about it. The wise have discussed various theories, as to whether God makes a white and a black man from the same original parents, or developes him from the lower animals.

The last thing any man will give up is his utter and total incompetency to do anything for his own salvation. There is nothing like answering a fool according to his folly. If a man comes and asks me how he is to carry five tons of coal on his back, I would not argue with him, I would give him half-an-hour to try it, and let that answer his own question.

The last thing we give up, is the thought that we can do something. Now, the first step is to accept God's record of us, not our opinion of ourselves. We have got to have faith in God's record of what man is, and faith in God's record of what He is, and it is said "the just shall live by faith." He has weighed us in the balance. We may think ourselves of some importance. Paul, when his eyes were opened, instead of climbing up the mighty elevation of self-confidence, went down into the deepest valley of humiliation, not singing the self-sufficient solo at the top of the mountain, but he is down in the depth. It is a bass solo, O Paul, you are singing, and not at all highly strung. What have you now? I have a revelation. "This is a faithful saying, and worthy of all acceptation, that Christ Jesus came into the world to save sinners." That is a saying and a beautiful saying too. It is sayings we go by, not feelings.

A photographer told me once that he had an order for six dozen photographs, by touching up the negative that was refused by a young man, who thought the original not nice enough. But an ugly truth is much better than a pretty falsehood. The truth, although it is ugly, is still truth in the end. Falsehood, though beautiful, is false in the end. Let us have the truth, whatever comes of it. God always likes to have a man confess his sins; He likes to have truth in the inward parts.

People must come down from the mountain of self-conceit and take God's opinion of themselves. God's photograph of you is full size from the crown of your head to the sole of your foot. We are "full of wounds, and bruises, and putrefying sores." How would you like that in your album and write under it,— "That's me." You don't know how the glory of God shines upon you, and diagnoses you. You know nothing about self. You know nothing about Christ's love, because you have never accepted the saying of the revelation of the truth of God, "And the just shall live by faith." I know I address some who say, I have by the grace of God found out by God's Word, and bitter experience that I am undone. Praise God, that is the right step to take.   Lie down and say, I need a Saviour.   It is not, "Who shall ascend into heaven?   That is to bring Christ down from above; nor, Who shall descend into the deep? that is, to bring Christ up."   One night I was trying to reach along the coast of England in a yacht; we could not weather the point, and our good captain said we would have to go under the lee, and cast anchor; and having let out a long length of chain— we had to do that because there was such a storm blowing— our men got ready, and when they were cleared they said, "Let go the anchor."   I did not see any one open the hatches and lower the anchor into the hold.   That is what your "feeling" people attempt to do, they lower it into the hold.   They won't let it go outside.   If I could feel some sensation coming over me and telling me I am saved, they say, I would be satisfied.   My anchor is Christ.   My anchor cannot fail until His power, and my Bible fail.   I shall anchor fast to the eternal Rock of Ages, and stand the storm, and live by faith.   "The just shall live by faith" (Gal. iii. 11).

There is nothing like making a good start.   Start well and start fair; that is, take the place that God has given you, in the ditch, and there you will find a good Samaritan having come all the way to you.

The Epistle to the Romans is justification by faith.   The Epistle to Galatians is justification by faith alone.   This faith is characterized by three things in the living—dependence, obedience, and (it leads to) experience.   Dependence, trusting upon God day after day.   Obedience, "If ye love Me, keep My commandments."   This life is essentially a life of obedience, dependence, and experience.   Our life goes on from day to day in a condition of dependence.

Remember, the bread of yesterday will not do for to-day. We must gather the manna fresh day after day, and the water the same way.

We sometimes hear of such and such an evangelist living by faith; such and such a philanthropist.   It may be in greater or less measure we live by faith.   But all believers live by faith.   For instance, here is a man that sends $3000, we will suppose, for some charitable purpose.   His giving is by faith.   The gifts of faith are as real as its receipts.   We must live by faith in the highest sense of the word.   Day after day we have to grow in this life.   We are told that we are to "renew our strength," if we wait upon the Lord, depending, and confiding, and trusting in Him. How is this accomplished? First "we mount up on wings as eagles." Now and then we see people who have received this sudden inspiration at conversion, start up and think they are in the seventh heaven. Don't clip their wings sooner than you can help it, let them speed toward the sky. They will know what it is to come back to earth and run by faith the "race that is set before them." Christian living, not talking, but Christian waiting and living; running the Christian race, and even *walking* and not fainting.

It is not every one who will go to the cave of Adullam with rejected David. Let us stand by him in adversity. "Yes, having done all, to stand." It sometimes takes all our strength and time to stand. It is all right in the revival times, in large meetings; but let us go away to our little fields, our small corners, with every one against us, and everything against us; then, having done all, to stand has something very grand in it. The grace that will make you full, will make you stand. "My grace is sufficient for thee;" and after this the Master will come to you and say: "You have been going about getting experience; you have come here; you have been failing, and you have been running, and you have been walking, and you have been standing; and I will make you to lie down." "He makes me to lie down," but it is among the green pastures and the still waters." A shepherd once said to me, "Did you ever see a sheep that was hungry lying down in green pastures? Not a bit of it; it is only the satisfied sheep that lies down in green pastures."

Finally, we must turn to the last passage, and we shall come to the words, "The just shall live by faith," in the 10th chapter of Hebrews. There is a future, as well as the past and present, and He that keeps me calm and patient, also keeps me looking to the right place for the reward. Emotionalism and sensationalism will not last. We must do our own little, calm work here, and look forward for a reward hereafter. We look forward, not to borrow to-morrow's troubles. If you wish to know the meaning of Christianity, don't borrow to-morrow's troubles. There will always be a way out of it. We know not the path, but we know the guide; and

> "The guide who led me hitherto
> Will guide me to the end."

We have been too long looking at the working side of life, instead of the outcome of life. Were you ever in a manufactory where pianofortes are made? Of all places in the world, don't go there for good music. I have been there, and of all the places of discord—tuning, tuning, tuning, and thump, thump, thumping, you ever heard,—it is dreadful. But if you want music, go to the band, and orchestra in its force. Down here is the place for tuning and making the instruments. By-and-by we shall have such a concert to the glory of our God; every one of us, small and big instruments, sounding to His praise and glory.

"The just shall live *by faith,*" *to the glory of God.*

THE CHRISTIAN WORKING ON THE EARTH.

"*And he said unto them, It is not for you to know the times or the seasons, which the Father hath put in his own power. But ye shall receive power, after that the Holy Ghost is come upon you: and ye shall be witnesses unto me both in Jerusalem, and in all Judea, and in Samaria, and unto the uttermost part of the earth.*"—ACTS i. 7, 8.

THE CHRISTIAN WORKING ON THE EARTH.

WE read in the first chapter of the Acts of the Apostles, just before our Lord left this world to go to glory, "It is not for you to know the times or the seasons, which the Father hath put in His own power; but ye shall receive power, after that the Holy Ghost has come upon you, and ye shall be witnesses unto Me, both in Jerusalem and in all Judea, and in Samaria, and to the uttermost part of the earth. And . . . He was taken up, and a cloud received Him out of their sight." Three parties are spoken of—the Holy Spirit, God, and Christ. These are the three persons most interested in carrying out God's work on earth. They are at the foundation, and the laying on of the top stone in Christian work.

"God sent forth His Son, born of a woman, born under the law, to redeem those who were under the law." Christ was sent from glory to perform the work of redemption—to fulfil the law of God, and put away sin, and to redeem us. He was God's witness on this earth, displaying the majesty of His law and the fulness of His grace. Who are the witnesses of God now? "Ye shall be witnesses unto Me in Jerusalem and in all Judea, and in Samaria, and to the uttermost part of the earth." We are the witnesses, commissioned from the throne of the eternal God. That word "sent" has much in it. It implies in the first place, distance. In the second place, it implies activity or energy. In the third place, it implies purpose, intention, design. We are as sheep far from home, out on the mountain; but the Shepherd was sent into the world from such a distance to save us. All the distance from heaven to earth has been covered by the "sent" one. God, in the strength of His own strong pity, in the energy of His holy love, sent His

Son to do the work which was to be done.   The sinner did not ask God to send His Son; but God sent His Son unasked for, and in wondrous grace, and He is now bringing many sons to glory, not only the Son in whom He was so well pleased, but the sons for whom He was offered up for the remission of sins, and offered on the cross as the first-fruits.   His purpose is, *we* shall be members of one body.

We take up now in our Christian work this peculiar mission. I am trying to get at the reason of our existence as Christian workers here; that which the world knows nothing about. The world knows something about philanthropy and morality, but our subject is not that to-day,—our subject is Christian work.   It is something heavenly and divine, not human; something eternal and not of time.   We come now to talk about Christian work, and that which separates it from all work, and that which is peculiar to it as *Christian* work, "Ye shall be witnesses unto Me."   We know of nothing that so ennobles men as Jesus Christ and Him crucified.   I don't say anything against philanthropy, nor against morality, for there is not any real or deep morality in fact, except that which springs from Christianity.   But morality does not go far enough. I don't think all our Christianity is absorbed where mere morality is preached.   How often the philanthropists of the world speak slightingly of the position assumed by Christianity in regard to philanthropic work.   But are they right, when in Christian lands alone, are to be seen the noble institutions for the relief of the sick, the out-growth of the teaching of Christianity, and supported by Christian men.   But there is something higher than mere philanthropy in Christianity.   What is it? "Ye shall be witnesses unto Me."

Look at the Christian's work.   First, the object for this work. We have a great work to do, but we have also a great power to perform our work with.   If I send my little boy to blow up five tons of solid rock, and give him a small chisel and a tack-hammer, it would be a long time before that rock was blown to pieces, but if you get a hole drilled, and put in dynamite or some other explosive agency, the rock soon gives way before that explosive agent.   The Lord gives you and me a great work to do, but with that work He has given us a great power to go forward with.   "Ye shall be witnesses unto Me, when ye shall receive power from the Holy Ghost."   We have received the Spirit of God not to keep it to ourselves, but that from us rivers of living water might flow.   Before all things, we are to be men of God.   The world knows nothing about this, and in the unrest, and weary work, and rushing hither and thither, and striving to out-do one another, they know little about the Great Spirit who is carrying out His purposes now.   You read early history and there you find the rise and fall of nation after nation.   You find the Jew giving place to the Babylonian, the Babylonian giving place to the Persian, the Persian giving place to the Greek, and the Greek giving place to the Roman, and dynasty after dynasty treading after the other, and wars and bloodshed, and all sorts of evil passing across this world; but faith rises above all these little points, and stands firm from eternity to eternity, and takes its stand with God, and says, "As for me, I wish to manifest God upon this earth."

Very soon you grow to look upon things according to your own standpoint.   On the top of the high hill things look very insignificant.   God says we must look at His work from His own point of view.   If every one were endued with a sense of his own littleness, he would see that the great things of the world are but as a speck in the eye of God.   Our determination then, should be that our work should be done, not by spasmodic efforts, and fits and starts, but to put it thus: "For to me to live is Christ."

Above all things we desire to be practical.   Perhaps you may forget all else, but there is one thing I want you to try and remember.   When alone in your own closet, before God, you may take a sheet of paper and put upon it, "For to me to live is ———." What?   Go on your knees for five minutes and see what it is. Some people's religion seems to be like a beautiful rose to be put on the coat and worn on special occasions.   That is not the life-work and that is not the working-life of Christianity. Let your Christian life be more than mere profession and sentiment.   It was the *false* prophet that said, "Let me die the death of the righteous, and let my latter end be like his."

Go to a working man who has to work with his hands.   You see him get up early on Monday morning, and he says he is going to work.   You ask him why he is working; he looks at you suspiciously and says, "I must work in order to get money." Your work is indeed changed into money—what is the use of money?   Money, sir, I must get money to get my food.

Food? what is the use of food? Why it is to get strength?
What is the use of strength? Why! that we may be able to
work. Oh, you are back at the first corner again. This is
your round—work, money, food, strength. Work, money, food,
strength, all over the world. The rich man's condition is far
worse. Instead of the work he has got laziness, and money,
and indigestion, and I don't think his condition is any better.
The Christian must take his place in his work and say, " I have
set the Lord always before me." "For to me to live is Christ."

What is it that peculiarly distinguishes the Christian's work
from other work? The Christian's work is the work of faith.
His life is the life of faith, and so is his work a work of faith.
It is not the work of the philanthropist, or the work of the mere
moralist, but it is the work of faith. The two works of faith
mentioned in the Word of God are most beautiful and wonderful works,—most peculiar works, I might say. In the Epistle
of James, we find that Abraham wrought a work of faith and
was justified. Rahab wrought a work of faith and was also
justified. Abraham's work was his intention to slay his son,
Isaac, the son of promise. What was Rahab's work? To
betray her country. Now infidelity comes and throws these
things in our face, and says, "What is the use of this kind of
work?" We stick to the word of truth, and know how to use
the sword that will not only be able to capture the gun from the
enemy, but be able to turn it against him, and let him have the
full force of it as he runs from the field. Never spike the
enemy's gun, but take it from him. Before all things we need
the Bible. You can't command people's consciences by order.
You can't feed people upon fig leaves ; you must give them
strong meat that they may grow thereon.

The works of faith mentioned in the Bible were works for
God, only so far as they had faith in them. Strip them of
faith, and they were not only immoral and unfeeling, but they
would have been sinful. The thing that characterizes the
works of God is faith in them. Abraham had faith in order to
have slain his son Isaac. If you asked Abraham if he had any
feelings when he was asked to slay his son, he would have
said: " I have feelings, but I have also faith. Every feeling of
my heart goes against it, but I am to do a work of faith, and
perform what God tells me to do, and therefore all my feelings
and sentiments must give way to the Great Law Giver, for

whom alone I work and to whom alone I listen." We must remember our own work, and must not think of another man's work. Every man has his own work to do. No other Christian can do your work. I have my work to do, and no other being in all heaven and earth can do it for me. You are the same. Christian, you have a work to do that none other can do, for God keeps no duplicates. No two beings are alike, and no two works in the great work of God are alike.

We regard the small stones in the temple as well as the large ones. A small stone can go where a large one would have to be cut down to fit. Some Christian people are often wishing to do something heroic, and to be seen. There are two classes of believers, those in the Christian work that are building what seems to be great in quantity, but precious little worth in quality. It is what we do and how we do it, that makes it acceptable to God. There is some of this work that is called gold, and some of it hay, and some of it stubble. I would rather have the gold than any amount of hay, and especially if there should be a fire, for the fire is to try all men's work; and if that is so, I would rather go in for the gold and silver and precious stones. We are to build the temples of God that will arise up to His glory in the endless ages, where all the wood, and hay, and stubble will be burned up in one great conflagration. Let our work be that which will survive the conflagration.

Build the greatest monuments of earth, and have the greatest number of jewels that you please, it is only to be added to the great conflagration at the end. "The earth shall be dissolved, and the elements shall melt with fervent heat." Get something that will not be burned. The beauty of real Christianity is this: none will sing a louder hallelujah than the believers themselves over the hay and stubble, and reserve the gold and silver to the glory of God. The best way for us all to do our work, is for us to do it ourselves; if each man does his work thoroughly, and each one sticks to his own place— has found out his place and sticks to it—and finds out his work and does it, then the great Christian work will go on.

In the coral reefs in the southern seas you see the corals working. They don't ask if the other is doing its work; they don't appoint committees to see if they are all working. They each work along and build up those great barriers and reefs. They are unconscious, but not unworthy instruments by which a hand invisible rears magnificent structures in the mysterious deep. Look at wrestling Jacob. I believe Jacob's wrestling was his weakness. God in His grace would make him His witness. A man wrestled with him, and he had to put his thigh out of joint before he could get him to his senses.

Just one word more. One great hindrance, if not the greatest hindrance that I know of, is this. I draw your attention to a passage in the Gospel according to Luke, the 9th chapter. Christ called his twelve disciples, "and gave them power and authority over all devils, and to cure diseases, and He sent them to preach the kingdom and heal the sick;" and so on. They got authority over all devils, and diseases, without exception. The next thing you hear of them is, a poor man brought his son to have a devil cast out of him. They had all authority, and it was not a question of Divine power. They had authority given to them. Why had they not power to do it? They had no faith. But why did they not have faith? Read on and you will find where the secret of it lies: "Then there arose a reasoning among them, which of them should be greatest." That is the point. Is it the case with us? The Lord help us to examine our work, and see if "for to us to live is Christ" or self.

OUR CONSECRATION AS PRIESTS UNTO GOD.

"*Ye also, as lively stones, are built up a spiritual house, an holy priesthood, to offer up spiritual sacrifices, acceptable to God by Jesus Christ.*

But ye are a chosen generation, a royal priesthood, an holy nation, a peculiar people : that ye should shew forth the praises of him who hath called you out of darkness into his marvellous light."—1 PETER ii. 5, 9.

OUR CONSECRATION AS PRIESTS UNTO GOD.

SOMETIMES we can understand a building better if we see the plans. In a large building with many rooms, corridors, and recesses, we are apt to get confused, and it is very convenient to get the plans and study them, when we can see our way about the house itself better than before. Now, that is just why we go back to the Book of Leviticus, in order that we may get the plans of the New Testament, and see the plans upon which its doctrines are reared.

Hence the absurdity of those who go back to copy the Old Testament ritual. It is just as if you have engaged a contractor to build a house for you, and when the day comes for him to give you the keys, he presents you with a nice bundle of plans, and says, "There's the house." That is absurd! Well, so it is with those who go back to the old ritual. Now we have the house, and although we look at the plans it is simply that we may understand the house better, and not that we may copy them. Thus it is that in the details of the New Testament teachings, we get many precious lessons from Leviticus.

The subject under consideration is, "priests unto God;" but I dare not attempt to enter upon this vast subject; I can scarcely deal even with one department of it; but I will try to call your attention to a few thoughts upon the consecration of priests, as shown in the types of the 8th chapter of Leviticus.

We all know well that Christ is the great High Priest of the Bible. He has spoken of us such, specially in the Book of Hebrews—that Book of which we are not told who was the writer. Theologians are divided as to who wrote it—some say Paul and some Apollos, but we have no key to the human hand that was used to write it. It begins as no other Epistle does—"God, who at sundry times," &c.   It is from Himself; and the child of God who reads it, is led in the third chapter to consider Jesus Christ as his Apostle and High Priest.   Only in the Epistle to the Hebrews is He called the Apostle.   The Apostle, not only coming from God to man, but also now appearing in the presence of God for man.

Now, it is generally allowed that we are Christ's representatives on earth; we appear before men as witnesses for God. The converse of this is also true, and we, as priests, appear before God for man.   We are priests unto God, and through the grace of Jesus Christ we have the power of intercession. We stand as ministers and officiating priests before Him, offering sacrifices daily unto His name.   Sacrifices have never ceased.   We are offering them day by day before the throne of grace.   And it is just because we have left this great truth out of sight that spurious sacrifices are so continually offered. We ought to be offering the sacrifice of praise continually.

He hath made us kings and priests unto God; we are made nigh by the blood, brought into the Holy of Holies, the veil rent, and therefore *no veil between*.   Thus we are in the brightest Shekinah of the glory of God; and this, remember, is not the privilege of a few Christians, but of all who are in Christ. It is our normal place.

We are not merely out of Egypt by faith in Christ; not merely through the desert by faith in Him; not merely into Canaan by faith; not merely entered into the holy place by faith; but into the holy place without a veil between.   That is the place of *all* who are in Christ; through Him who has entered by His own blood into the heavens, there to appear in the presence of God for us.

Thus, when we read of Aaron, we have a type of Christ as the great High Priest; when we read of Moses, we have a type of Christ as the Great Prophet; and, when together with these we have the elders spoken of, we have a type of Christ as our King.   So, in Leviticus, we have Christ shown forth as Prophet, Priest, and King.   And thus, in the eighth chapter, we have the manifestation of Christ Himself, and of the provision He has made for us.

I cannot go into this wonderful chapter in detail, but to you who study your Bibles, I will give a few hints, that you may find out these precious truths for yourselves.

First, then, we have here Aaron as representing the great High Priest. In the first thirteen verses of the chapter we have this consecration spoken of; but, when we come to the fourteenth verse, we find there is a sin-offering. This refers to our priesthood. Before there can be consecration we have two most important sacrifices to be offered. First, the sin-offering, and then the burnt-offering for a sweet savour. That is a lesson to anyone who may be wishing to do anything for the Lord, to consecrate his time, his talents, his money, or his service to the Lord. Till he come to the cross there can be no consecration. Whatever he may do, it is but dead works. He may even give his body to the flames, in the hope that there will arise to God the incense of a sweet savour. But, no, no! till there be a sin-offering, there can be *no* consecration.

The place of the sin-offering. And remember the place of sin-offering is far away—outside the camp. A man may come offering his money; but no, it cannot be accepted until he has taken his place as a poor sinner—outside the camp. "What," he says, "must I go away beyond the tribe of Dan?" Yes, you must go past their camp—they are nearest the place of sin-offering. The publicans and sinners are nearest it, and it is easiest for them to take their proper place. It is hard for the self-righteous to go there; but until they have been there their service cannot be acceptable to Him. We must be clear about this.

Have we gone in the consciousness of our own guilt, outside the camp, and there seen our guilt placed upon Christ, and learned that we, as sinners, are saved through His blood? If you have not been there, then the sooner you go the better. "Behold, now is the accepted time; behold now is the day of salvation." Cain tried to leap through all these barriers, and to be a worshiper at once. He came with the beautiful fruits of the earth ere he brought the blood; but to his offering God had not respect. So with you, if you have not been to the sin-offering your sacrifice is in vain.

But now, after the sin-offering, where the victim is identified with the sin of the offerer, we have the burnt-offering for a sweet smelling savour. And thus we find Christ offered Himself for our sins, and also for a sweet smelling savour—an offering without spot or blemish. And we have all the virtue of the glorious fulness of Christ. All that He is, I am. All His

goodness is put to my account.   Just as I am identified with
Him in death, so in resurrection ; and thus I am not only
absolved from guilt, but also accepted in the Beloved.   Not
only are our sins put away, but we are in the risen One—
standing in Him.

And thus God can smile upon us without compromising His
glory.   He cannot put the consecrating oil upon an uncleansed
or unworthy sinner ; but in Christ I am worthy—worthy in Him
alone.   All His work is mine, and thus standing in Him, I am
of the blood-royal of heaven,—"accepted in the Beloved,"
complete in Him."   And now, after all this, God comes down
with the consecrating oil and blood.

Now, then, we can pass on, the sin and burnt-offering being
past, to the consecration of priests.   From the twenty-second
verse to the close of the chapter, as also the few closing verses
of the following chapter, will be found profitable reading on
this subject.

We have three thoughts about consecration here.   First, we
have the blood (the blood first), and the oil of consecration ;
second, the basket of consecration ; and third, the place of
consecration.

We sometimes hear about Christians *consecrating themselves*
to the Lord.   Well, this is right enough in a modified sense.
But I believe in scriptural expressions, such as, "Yield yourselves unto God, as those that are alive from the dead, and your
members as instruments of righteousness unto God."

In these Old and New Testament words, the great work of
consecration is kept in the Lord's hand.   He alone can consecrate us, if the consecration is to be valid.   In His consecration
I find power and strength.   It is not the meeting of a few friends
and others, who say, "I will consecrate myself to the Lord,"
where true consecration is to be found ; but it is when the Lord,
by His Spirit, comes and shines into my soul, and says, "You
are consecrated already—the blood is upon you, the oil is upon
you ; ye are not your own, ye are bought with a price."   Then
we are consecrated.   God has made us kings and priests to Him
and has consecrated us to Himself.   It is that alone which
makes us rise to the full dignity of our priesthood, and dare to
bear testimony for God before our fellow-men.   It would be no
use for me to say that I can take upon me the duties of the
Home Minister, and to go to the Home Office, and say I will

put everything right. Why, stop till you are put into the Home Office, and then try to do your best. It is when a man is put into a certain office, that he rises up, or ought to rise up, saying, "I will do the duties of that office properly."

And so here; it is not I who consecrate myself to the Lord, but it is He who has taken me from the "miry clay, and set my feet upon a rock, and established my goings." And not only so, He has made me His witness upon earth. "I am not my own, I am bought with a price."

There is just now too much of we! we! We do this or that; we consecrate ourselves. Let us get rid of this doing, and remember that it is not we, but it is the Lord. Through Christ "we are accepted in the Beloved," and the oil and the blood has been put upon me by God Himself.

This consecration is not to be confounded with moral progressive sanctification, which is so necessary to us all. That goes on day by day, and week by week, in calm, steady continuance in well-doing. But this consecration is done by Himself once for all. Of His own will He has consecrated us, once for all, to Himself. From the very day of our separation to Him, on the day when we first came to Him and had our sins put away, and were made priests unto Him, we have been consecrated to the Lord.

Oh, how many of us have been groping about when that thought should have raised us from the earth. We have been living as earth-born, instead of heaven-born men. It is even as if we had been in heaven, and sent back to earth to be witnesses for Him. The cross of Christ has taken us out of the world, and by His resurrection we have been sent back to the earth to testify for Him.

It is, then, for you, fellow priests unto God—for all God's children are priests—it is for you to forget the things that are behind, to let them pass with old years, and now to start as heaven-born priests. Let us rise and take our position and standing as priests unto God; to see the blood upon my ear, and therefore I listen to no communication that is not in accordance with the Word; to see the blood upon my hand, and therefore I touch nothing that is not for the glory of God; to see the blood upon my feet, and therefore I will go nowhere, and mix with no society, where I cannot testify for Him. Thus have we the "beauty of holiness."

We might well tremble if we found that consecration was only by the blood. For, while blood stands for atonement, it has also a deeper meaning. What does it stand for here? It signifies that we are wholly His, that we are *bought*. It is the measure of our consecration. One man may be much exercised as to how much he shall give to the Lord. Shall it be a tenth? even as the godly Jew gave a tenth to the Lord. Or shall it be nine-tenths, or this or that amount? Oh, friends, this settles all—"Ye are not your own." And though we have not yet resisted unto blood, nor are we called upon at the present day, yet we are *wholly* His—life, treasure, all I have and all I am, belong to Him, and not a part only. The whole of our being, right on to death—spirit, soul, and body, right to the end of life, belong to God.

That is what we are called to as priests unto God. And this is the reason the oil is put upon us. The oil signifies the Spirit which is given us, that we may follow Christ in His utter abandonment of self, and His full devotion of service for life and for death. Consecrated with the oil, the whole of our life must be utter and entire unselfishness—continually imitating Christ, not only simply doing our duty, but following Him who gave Himself for us.

The second thought here is, that this consecration by blood and oil, is fed and nourished at "the basket of consecration." What was the food that our blessed Master fed upon? for we must always look to Him as the great model. He said to His disciples, when they returned from buying bread, and pressed Him to eat, "I have meat to eat that ye know not of." What was that meat? "To do the will of Him that sent me, and to finish His work." Now this is what we are to feast upon continually. One feast will not do. The basket was to provide food for *all* the days of consecration. And, as we need our daily bread for the support of the temporal body, so we need the divine food for the support of our consecrated nature; and that food is nothing more than doing His will. Just as we are following Him, and are content to give up our own will, whatever it may cost, so will we be nourished and strengthened.

And, remember, this is not one act, but a continual going on, on, in serving and following Him. We must seek to know His will, not our own. Remember, that we have much to contend with in this world. Why? Because there is not a

Christian man or woman who has not in them something older than their spiritual life.   In other words, the old nature is older than the new.   Some of you were twenty years old when you started the new life; by that time a young man has all his plans for his future life laid.   These plans were laid before his consecration, and it is natural that with the new life should come an entire change.   Yet, many of us are continuing in our daily life to follow out our old purposes.   Thus, perhaps, some of you are working, or business men, who should be missionaries, or preachers.

Let us be feeding upon the will of the Lord, and resigning ourselves entirely to His will.   Let us seek to know His will, —"Lord, what would'st thou have me to do?"   Month by month, and year by year, let us seek to know His will, and His alone.   This is feeding from the "basket of consecration."

Lastly, we are to abide at the door of the tabernacle, and keep the charge of the Lord.   We are here as His witnesses, keeping His charge.   He Himself said, "For their sakes I sanctify myself, that they also might be sanctified through the truth."   Christ was separated from all His glory and possessions, while on earth, in order that He might have us waiting for Him *when He comes.*

These, then, are our days of consecration.   We are passing along surely to the end.   We know not the hour, but we know that we are a year nearer the glory, than a year ago.

Eighteen centuries ago, He said, "Behold, I come quickly;" and yet here we are waiting still.   What have we to do whilst waiting?   What is our place?   Keeping the charge of the Lord.   "What I say unto you, I say unto all, Watch."   Why?   Because we "know not the hour when the Son of Man cometh."   Let us keep His command—abiding His will— waiting for His presence.   It is thus that we shall fulfil the days of consecration.

What, then, have we been doing?   Alas, alas, none of us have risen to this glorious privilege!   He has told us to keep His commands.   His last command was, "Go ye, therefore, and teach all nations, baptizing them in the name of the Father, and of the Son, and of the Holy Ghost; teaching them to observe all things whatsoever I have commanded you.   And, lo, I am with you alway, even unto the end of the world."

That was His last command, and yet a hundred years have

scarcely elapsed since Christians began to think that the heathen should be looked after at all, or told the story of the cross!
And, at this moment, more than half the globe has never heard
of His name.   Yet we, who are priests unto God, and pledged
to do His will, and keep the charge of the Lord, stay at home
at ease, and keep our money in our pockets when demands are
made for the help of those who have gone.   Is this carrying
out His will? which is beautifully expressed in the hymn—

> " Send the blessed tidings all the world around;
> Spread the joyful news wherever man is found,
> Whosoever will may come."

Shall we not, then, rise up at once as those who are
waiting for the full manifestation of His glory?   Let us be
waiting at His door, looking for the time when all shall fall on
their faces before Him.   Brethren, the days are few.   Soon
shall He come whose right it is to reign; and then, amid brighter glories than ever man in his wildest dreams thought of, we
shall *see* Him in the glory, and shall be hailed with, "Well
done, good and faithful servant."   Not for the success we have
met with, but that we have been keeping His charge.

Many are at home in quiet corners, who ought to be out to
every place under the sun, spreading His name.   Oh, brethren,
we are priests !   We, who have come to Christ as the sin-offering, who have known Him as the burnt offering of a sweet-
smelling savour, who have had the blood and the oil put upon
us, the charge of the Lord is upon us to keep His commands,
and the provision for our need is there.   Oh, let us be stead-
fast, immovable, always abounding in every good work, abiding
at the door of the tabernacle, "For He that shall come will
come, and will not tarry."   And remember, that in the day of
the full blaze of the manifested glory of the Lord, if a regret
were possible amidst that glory, it will be that we have done
so little to "keep the charge of the Lord."

PRIEST AFTER THE ORDER OF MELCHISEDEC

" *For he testifieth, Thou art a priest for ever, after the order of Melchisedec.*"—HEBREWS vii. 17.

" *For this Melchisedec, king of Salem, priest of the most high God, who met Abraham returning from the slaughter of the kings, and blessed him ; To whom also Abraham gave a tenth part of all ; first being, by interpretation, King of righteousnees, and after that also, King of Salem, which is, King of peace ; Without father, without mother, without descent, having neither beginning of days, nor end of life ; but, made like unto the Son of God, abideth a priest continually.*"—HEBREWS vii. 1-3.

PRIEST AFTER THE ORDER OF MELCHISEDEC.

WE are now to speak of the Melchisedec priesthood of the Lord Jesus Christ, and to that end let us read the Word of God upon it, in Heb. vii., "For this Melchisedec, king of Salem, priest of the most high God, who met Abraham returning from the slaughter of the kings, and blessed him; to whom also Abraham gave a tenth part of all; first being by interpretation King of righteousness, and after that also King of Salem, which is, King of peace; without father, without mother, without descent, having neither beginning of days, nor end of life; but made like unto the Son of God; abideth a priest continually." "Now"—and mark the Divine exhortation—"consider how great this man was, unto whom even the patriarch Abraham gave the tenth of the spoils. And verily, they that are of the sons of Levi, who receive the office of the priesthood, have a commandment to take tithes of the people according to the law, that is, of their brethren, though they come out of the loins of Abraham. But he whose descent is not counted from them, received tithes of Abraham." This is the true explanation of that—"Without father or mother." It is, that his descent is not counted. His descent is not reckoned as from the ordinary line of the priesthood. He received tithes from Abraham, "and blessed him that had the promise"—two wonderful marks of superiority—got tithes from Abraham, and blessed Abraham, "and without all contradiction, the less is blessed of the better." Now, the position that we take in considering how great this man was, is this, that all that we have heard of the Aaronic priesthood, and of the mediatorial kingship, merely goes by a process of a *fortiori* reasoning in the consideration of the greatness of Christ in the

Melchisedec function.   That He, the king and the priest united in one man, absorbs all that was seen, and much greater
than all that is seen, either in the Divinie or the mediatorial
reign, so-called, or in the Aaronic priesthood.   Christ is the
order of Melchisedec, and not of Aaron.   He performs all the
functions now of the Aaronic priesthood ; but, sin being in the
way, and sin being in the question, requires sacrifices from
man to God, and, if we turn back to the original account of
Melchisedec, we find there was no sacrifice mentioned in
connection with Melchisedec's blessing Abraham.   There was
no incense.   There is no hope from any sacrifice to God
there.   And if we look at the priesthood in the various ways in
which God is manifested to man, we will learn very much of
the blessed teaching of the Lord Himself.   Perhaps it may not
seem to be what people call "practical."   People are always
talking about what is "practical."   "Let us have," they say,
"what is practical."   I often ask the question, "Whether do
you mean, practical from God's point of view, or practical from
your own point of view ?"   When Abraham was taken into
the confidence of God about Lot, he never uttered a word
about himself.   It was all interceding for Lot.   "And shall I
hide from My friend Abraham what is going to come upon his
nephew Lot, in Sodom ?"

My friends, we must be, if we are in God's mind, we will be
—interested in God's truth because it is God's.   We may rise
up to it if we say, "Give us this day our daily bread," but we
will be eating the old corn of the land, instead of the finest of
the wheat.   God is not for Himself and in Himself.   What
God in His majesty, in His might, in His history in the past, in
the present, and to come, in a past eternity, in a present dispensation of time, in the glory; and in the coming glory—all is
from the Godward point of view, and we will all find it practical
to the glory of Him whose name is put above every name.   If
we look at the patriarchal time, we see this first, and the first
shall be last.   That which was first found in the seed-plot of
Genesis will be the development of the glory that is the last
of the dispensations.   The Melchisedec priesthood and kingship
that came first representing the last before the roll of time is
wrapped up.   We there find when the servant was coming from
the wars, as in the Book of Exodus, the first scene recorded in
all history, whether sacred or profane, long before the Iliad of

Homer was sung, we find it was so when they were delivered from the Egyptian slavery. God for them destroyed their foes, and on the wilderness shore of the Red Sea they sang, as the first song of history, the song of redemption—and the first shall be last. And the first battle as recorded in history is the type of the last. The first shall be last again ; and the battle, the first that is recorded in profane or sacred history, is the battle at the close of which Melchisedec met Abraham. Melchisedec appears to him on his return, and does two things—the two proper things in connection with king and priest. As priesthood represents headship for man in things pertaining to God, and kinghood represents representation in rule of God over man. Melchisedec came thus with the provision, the nourishment, the refreshment, and joy of the king, and he did two things —he blessed Abraham from the Most High God, and he blessed the Most High God from Abraham. He had blessings rising up, and blessings flowing down; and we know when Jesus came in the 1st and 2nd chapters of John, before He shows how love is communicated to us on the earth, He gives us a glimpse of all His glories. In the 1st of John you will get all the personal and official glories of our Lord essentially portrayed, and in the 2nd chapter you get two wonderful acts symbolic of the Head, of His glory when there He purges the Temple; and of His power when He begins His series of miracles at Cana, where He turned that which is required to cleanse, into the wine of the kingdom, for the first shall be the last, and the water shall be the wine, and all shall rejoice when David is King, and the day of feasting is come. The Lord in partriarchal days (and Melchisedec shows the great thought) was God in heaven, and the worshipers and sacrificers were upon the earth, and the great thought is the glory of God in heaven, ministering to men —He as the Judge and the Ruler—here upon the earth with rebellious man. Or if, as it is said sometimes, as if to take the royal attributes from our Blessed Lord, that God is love, and would make such a sentiment a mockery of the Great and Holy God, as would make it appear that He had no authority, and no power, and no righteousness, and no holiness *to damn* —that is His own word—to kindle wrath, we have to ask another question and a prior question—What is God ? We have to ask who it is that is love ? Who is it ? It is not the senti-

ment of man.   It is the God that cannot live in the presence
of sin without punishing sin.   It is the God that cannot bear
sin because He is love.   It is the God of Calvary, whose own
Son when lying under it, had to say, " My God, my God, why
hast Thou forsaken Me ? "   It is the God who will have a solid
peace—a blessed peace.   Let it be war as it may be, for while
we may wish to take the easy texts of Scripture that may read
of the time when men should beat their swords into ploughshares, and their spears into pruning-hooks, I ask of you also
to study God on another side when He tells them to " Proclaim ye this among the Gentiles ; prepare war ; wake up the
mighty men ; let all the mighty men of war draw nigh ; let
them come up ; beat your *ploughshares* into swords, and your
pruning-hooks into spears."   God does not bless when sin has
been here, but through the judgment of sin ; that is, individually or nationally.   So the world wide ; *He cleanses always by
judgment.*   So, when His returning warrior, Abraham, who had
beaten his ploughshare into a sword, went away, leaving his
nomadic practices to betake himself to the new trade of warrior, the Most High God puts Himself near him, like some
wondrous strange flash never before seen, and never again to
be seen, after he has fulfilled the function of his type; and there
He blesses as the high priest, not of Jehovah and of a nation,
but of the Most High God, the possessor of heaven and earth.
Our Lord is called " King Jesus."   Our Lord is called "King
of kings."   Our Lord is called " King of nations."   Our Lord
is called " King of glory."   It is now conceded that the passage in Revelation "King of saints," is *Ethnol*, not *Hagnel*.   It
has to do with nations ; and His true, royal rights in connection with this earth are not seen until Israel is seen as the
centre, and the nations of the earth blessed in Him, calling
Him blessed.   Such is His true scriptural kingship—first seen
as God in the heavens, and man upon the earth a worshiper
with His sacrifice to the living God.   When we come now
to Exodus, or to Jewish times we find that the way is to
be seen, and God is found upon the earth and the
worshipers and the sacrifice upon the earth also; that He
makes, or gets man to make for Him, a dwelling-place upon
the earth, a tabernacle, and worshipers and sacrificers
are there to show the way of approach to Him.   Then when
we come to our dispensation, we find that God is in heaven,

but worshipers and sacrifice are there too.   We are seated in
the heavenly places, not *with* Christ yet, but *in* Christ, and there
is our standing in heaven, with boldness to draw near without
a veil between.   And in the glory that is to come, when Christ
takes His Kingship, then we will find that the heavens and the
earth are united, and God is in both heaven and earth, and as
His witnesses, and worshipers in the heavens and in the earth,
in the Church of God with His heavenly ones, and with the
Jew and the nations of the earth, and all the earth filled with
the knowledge of the Lord.   Then we have the characteristics
of God's kingship and priesthood as represented in Melchisedec.
It is a remarkable thing when we study this book of Hebrews,
which tells us of the way into the holiest—not the blessings of
the Melchisedec, but the blessings of Aaronic priesthood—we
never hear anything about a temple.   The word temple, or
that temple, is *never* found in Hebrews.   Just as when we
come to the study of the Book of Revelation, the thought of us
being the children of the Father is *never* in all Revelation
found.   He is never our Father in the Revelation.   He is the
Lord God Almighty, and the Lamb.   But the New Testament
Fatherhood is not taken up in the Revelation.   So in Hebrews.
There is not the temple, but the tabernacle, because it was the
pattern of things in the heavenlies that was given in the Book
of Hebrews, and the temple refers to an established state of
things in the land.   For in the Book of Exodus we have the
Priesthood in connection with the tabernacle, with all its furniture, symbolism, and the like.   Now, if you look at Exodus,
Leviticus, and Deuteronomy, we have the tabernacle in Exodus,
and where?   Where God was to be met.   In Leviticus, the
priest's service book ; in Numbers we get the kingdom, but as
a lamp in the wilderness; not a settled, and established, and
fixed thing in the land.   Then we have the condition in which
they were to be in the land, in the Book of Deuteronomy.
And so when we get to heavenly things themselves, in the Book
of Hebrews, it is all according to that which we have in the
wilderness making way.   Now when Christ has come and
finished the work ; when it is that He has done the work that
will put away sin and bring in everlasting righteousness, why
does He not at once step on to Melchisedec's throne ?   Why
is it that now He does not exercise the functions of the king
and of the priest evidently before the world ?

Ah! there comes in this wondrous silence, this wondrous pause, this wondrous drag upon the wheels of time, when God might have come down with one fell swoop on all the rejectors of His Son. Nay, He makes the wrath of man to praise Him, and He postpones Melchisedec's glory, that He may reveal from His own heart's love a more wondrous mystery that was hid in God from the foundation of the world; not blessing to a nation, or to a nation through a nation, but the middle wall of partition broken down, the new body, the bride of the Lamb gathered out of every nation, kindred, and tongue, to the glory of His blessed name, and receiving the royal glory there, "and He has not sat down on His throne," as He tells us. "To him that overcometh will I give to sit on My throne." His Father said, "If the world won't give you the throne as the Son of Man, and if the Jew won't give you the throne of David, I will set you at My right hand, I will give you a higher throne, and a better throne, a more wonderful throne than all, and that is why He is to convince the world of righteousness, because "I go to My Father." If the world is so unrighteous that they can't see any beauty in Him, and give Him nails instead of a sceptre, and thorns instead of glory, and mocking instead of worship; oh, He has a righteous Father, and the Father will reward Him for the travail of His soul even now, and the Father will show what a righteous, and a perfect man, and God-glorifying man, He was here upon earth. And He says, "Sit at My right hand, until I make My enemies Thy footstool." And so in this wonderful time that He spanned right over, and said, that He was coming back quickly (He does not say very *soon*, it is quickly), it is the heart of love; it is not the date of time, because you know that to a man on a dark night the nearest point is the lighthouse. He does not see hills, and valleys, and rivers, but the lighthouse. Keep looking forward to the lighthouse. It is the nearest point to us in the darkness of night, and His heart runs over all this pause when He is showing that wondrous thing—resurrection life. Risen men were not merely a number of people testifying on the earth of Jew and Gentile —but risen men, men identified with Him, standing at the Heaven-side of Jesus, at the resurrection side of the tomb—identified with the heavenly one, holy, heavenly men, living upon the earth. Such is our true character, if we would rise up to it. That would soon strip the jewels off you

—not that we are going to heaven all at once. It is not that we are earthly men, wishing to go to heaven : we are heavenly men sent back to earth, the witnesses for Him; for, mark you, before I can get into a place I must be out of it. "As Thou hast sent me into the world;" this is the root of all our worldliness. Some people say they don't like doctrine. I believe there is no practice without doctrine for its basis. A man's practice will never rise above his doctrine, and his doctrine just is to make everything as comfortable as he can, and get to heaven by the easiest practicable road. And so like a musty parchment, they shut up their title-deeds to heaven in a safe, fire-proof, judgment-proof, and hell-proof, and hope to get into heaven in the long run. Is that the resurrection life ? Is that "risen with Christ ?" Is that a "sent man"—as the Father sent Me into the world—the meaning being a "sent man." The cross of Christ takes us out of the world, and the resurrection of Christ sends us back a firebrand, with motives, principles, aims, ambitions, hopes, and joys that they cannot understand or comprehend where we got them from.

So thus in this little pause He has identified Himself with us in resurrection life. In the Melchisedec idea, the full truth of him in blessing was seen. In the Jewish priesthood the full idea of the way was seen. In the Christian dispensation the full idea of the life is seen, and you see all put together with Melchisedec, and Aaron, and Jesus. Now we have the way, the truth, and the life. Time fails us, but the glory won't. They that are Christ's at His coming will continue this subject in the Melshisedec glory that is then to be revealed; but we have the benefits of it now. So, just looking at the different methods in which our blessed Lord left us, we see that in John, where we have the manifestation of Him in all His perfection here upon the earth for us, it is never said that He went into heaven at all. There is no ascension in John. It says, as His parting words, "Follow Me"—to heaven, you see, is naturally implied. He is not to be separated from us. We are heavenly men by the admonition of John. His last words to Peter, John, and the rest, were, "Follow Me" —not a word about the cloud receiving Him.

In Mark, the beautiful little Gospel that tells us of this service, He shows that they would have miraculous power over evil, and adds : "So then after the Lord had spoken unto them,

He was received up into heaven, and sat on the right hand of God." In Matthew He gives His grand marching order. What a sensation the *Times* would cause if some morning it could say that in some of the low parts of London had been found the true heir of the House of Brunswick. You never heard such a commotion as that would cause, if it could be shown that by indisputable rights our blessed Queen should be deposed, and that the true King was found. We read Matthew as if it were a mere human prediction of names; but it is to prove His royal rights to the throne of His Father David, and do you think God will let them off when He has had the trouble to prove them? Do you think that we can spiritualize it into His spiritual throne, when He has taken great care to make it a genealogical throne. He has shown that He must reign as the successor to David, and He will do it, and at the end of that He gives us the great marching order—" Go ye into all the world and preach the Gospel to every creature," which, if we do not do, we will not get the privilege to do before the return of the Jews, for the Jews will do it in spite of us. That is what will happen. If we do not rise to the dignity of our call, it will be done by them. "This Gospel of the Kingdom shall be preached in all nations for a testimony;" but it may not be the privilege of the Church of God. Those godly Jews who have come through great tribulation may get the privilege.

> " From Greenland's icy mountains,
>   From India's coral strand.
> They call us to deliver
>   Their land from error's chain.
>
> " Shall we, whose souls are lighted
>   With wisdom from on high,
> Shall we, to men benighted,
>   The lamp of life deny? "

And so He gives us this commission in Matthew at His depart-ure ; but when, as the Son of Man and true Melchisedec, He is taken away, at the end of Luke's Gospel, what do we find it said of Him? Similar to what is said in Matthew : "And He led them out as far as Bethany, and He lifted up His hands and blessed them. And it came to pass, while He blessed them, He was parted from them, and carried up into heaven." The last look that the believing eye saw, was the uplifted hand

and the blessing left by their Friend ; gaze upon Him, for He goes that way.   The true Melchisedec—blessed be Abraham. The uplifted hands, the blessing, is for us.   I think that we shall be very much humbled when He tells us, " Lo, I am with you alway," to do the work.   He has never altered the attitude of blessing.   But oh ! how disobedient have we been in the line of service !   " I am with you."   My friend, *there* is the royal presence.   You talk about mimicking and aping Rome, with all its tomfoolery and flummery, and music, and machinery, and gymnastics.   You talk to them, and they will make it appear to you they have some royal presence.   My friend, off to China with you, off to Japan with you, with the living God alone at your back, and then you will realize the royal presence —" Lo, I am with you alway, to the end of the age."   And you will see Him in China, and in Japan, with uplifted hands, just as here, for it is the Son of Man, of Luke, it is the Melchisedec story—that He uplifted His hands, and as He was blessing them, He was caught up into heaven.   Brethren, there is a great danger in ever being taught the truth of God under some circumstances.   It is this, and it is a very subtle danger, that we are taken up more with the blessings that we get than with the Blessed Lord Himself—more with the little cup that is so cracked that it cannot hold the stream that is poured into it, than with the great fountain from whence the stream flows.   Mr. Moody used to say, " The only way to keep a broken vessel full is to keep it always under the tap."   Now that is it.   You need the tap to-morrow.   You can't live upon to-day's food to-morrow.   It breeds worms in the wilderness. There is no food kept over for to-morrow, but the Giver is there.   We are taken up more with what grace has done for us than the grace that has done it.   This is the subtle error, and a very subtle error, especially to those who are Christians and who have studied the Word of God.   We are taken up with the idea of our seat in the heavenlies, our comfort and joy, and singing and everything else, but not with Himself.   We must draw attention to error as well as to the knowledge of the truth. It must be with us as it was with the disciples on the Mount of Transfiguration :—"They saw no man save Jesus only." What could be more appropriate than to read 1 Chron. xii, in where we read that glorious lesson to men in such a state as we are now, when David had not his throne, just as where our Christ is now when He has not His throne—in a parenthesis—there is the similarity between the anointing and the crowning at Hebron, and the coronation at Jerusalem. So we are in the little interval while he yet keeps Himself close.   He was not the manifestation of the son of God, but "while He yet kept Himself close because of Saul" then we find the brave men gathered to him in the wilderness many men of war from among the Gaddites fit for the battle. We need that.   We need the Gaddites.   We need the men of war.   Romanism, Ritualism, and Spiritualism—are coming in like a flood; and, besides, we scarcely know the amount of open infidelity that is about us.   We need, therefore, the men of war able to "contend earnestly for the faith once delivered to the saints."   Then we require the Benjamites, "famous throughout the house of their fathers."   And there is another kind that we require—the children of Issachar, "who have understanding of the times."   There is so much misunderstanding of the times, that we are all adrift.   We have been trying to convert Britain, instead of, to evangelize the world.   These things should be done, but the others not left undone, and they would not be if we had "an understanding of the times." "They had an understanding of the times, to know what Israel ought to do, and all they their brethren were at their commandment."   They studied the times, and we should study the times by the light of God's Book.   All these were men of war, and there was one noticeable thing about them—they kept rank.   "They came with a perfect heart to make David king." And that is what we want—to make Christ King, that He may receive His royal rights as the Son of David, the Son of man, the Son of God, over the universe.   And they could keep rank. I fear we are bad soldiers in keeping rank.   When I was a volunteer, we had to be out at six o'clock in the morning practising to keep rank.   Hour after hour we went at it, and the young recruits were always falling out of rank.   I remember our sergeant used to go with his naked sword along the line to see that we "dressed up," as he called it.   Dress up, Christians; let us keep rank!   Do you know the way we did it?   We took our line from the left-hand or right-hand man, whoever might be in front.   Take your line, Christians, from the Captain.   Keep your eye upon Him, and dress up to His level.   Do not rush in front or lag behind.   Dress up!   Keep

rank! Have you any extra power as a believer? then go and
help the weak one to keep rank. Don't try to patronize a
fellow Christian, but try to dress him up and keep him in rank.
And do so with singleness of heart. We may differ on many
points. We do differ on many points, but we are one in Christ.
We could throw a bombshell into the middle of a meeting
in a moment, but the love of Christ constraineth us to avoid
this. We wish every heart to be filled with one thought,
absorbed with one feeling, which finds its expression in—

> " Worthy the Lamb that died, they cry,
>   To be exalted thus;
> Worthy the Lamb, our lips reply,
>   For He was slain for us."

We are all of a single heart, beloved. With all our failure,
ignorance, and aim, we have a single heart, and though we do
not all dress up as we ought to do, we have the single heart to
proclaim our David King. Yes, we are waiting for Him, not
that we may get away from the strife and the toil. We are not
all tired of the battle. We have with Paul the desire to depart
and to be with Him, which is far better, but not that we may
get comfortably away into nice easy-chairs, to sing the songs of
bliss, to wear the crowns of gold, and to have all tears wiped
away from our eyes, that is not what we are waiting for—
David to be king; for Him, my friends. It is that the Prince of
Darkness may be cast out; it is that the right may triumph
over the wrong; it is that righteousness may run through our
land, and through the world like a river, and not the ungodliness
of sin that is now polluting this fair earth. It is that Antichrist
may be cast down, Babylon destroyed, and truth triumph above
all error. It is that all that was lost by our first Adam may be
gathered up in the hands of the Son of man; that all that was
lost in the covenant with Noah, may be gathered up in the
hands of Him that is the Judge of all the earth. It is that
all that was lost in David and in Solomon's reigns, may be
gathered up in Him who will gather up and restore Ephraim
and Judah, and they shall sing of the same brotherly love in
the Temple of their God, "Behold, how good a thing it is for
brethren to dwell together in unity."

MY NAME'S SAKE.

"*And ye shall be hated of all men for my name's sake: but he that endureth to the end shall be saved.*"—MATTHEW x. 22.

"*But all these things will they do unto you for my name's sake, because they know not him that sent me.*"—JOHN xv. 21.

"*And hast borne, and hast patience, and for my name's sake hast laboured, and hast not fainted.*"—REV. ii. 3.

"MY NAME'S SAKE."

IMMEDIATELY after our Lord, in teaching His disciples how to pray, revealed to them their position as children, though still far from home, and thus warranted to address His Father as their Father, and say, " Our Father who art in heaven," He instructed them to add, "Hallowed be Thy name." We thus join in worship with all the loyal universe of God, animate and inanimate.

" Praise ye Him, all His ANGELS. Praise ye Him, all His hosts. Praise ye Him, sun and moon : praise Him all ye stars of light.

" Praise ye Him, ye HEAVENS of heavens, and ye waters that be above the heavens. Let them praise the name of the Lord.

" Praise the Lord from the EARTH, ye dragons, and all deeps : fire and hail, snow and vapours ; stormy winds, fulfilling His word ; mountains and all hills ; fruitful trees and all cedars ; beasts and all cattle ; creeping things and flying fowl : kings of the earth, and all people ; princes, and all judges of the earth : both young men and maidens ; old men and children : let them praise the name of the Lord ; for His name alone is excellent ; His glory is above the earth and heavens. . . . . Let everything that hath breath, praise the Lord. Praise ye the Lord."

While we are loving sons, we are devout worshipers, and take our stand beside the adoring living ones, who rest not day and night, saying, " Holy, holy, holy, Lord God Almighty, who was, and is, and is to come ;" and falling down before Him that sits on the throne, we worship Him that liveth for ever and ever, and cast our crowns before the throne, saying, " Thou art worthy, O Lord, to receive glory, and honour, and power ; for Thou hast created all things, and for Thy pleasure they are and were created." And deeper still does our worship reach as we enter into the hall of redemption, for we can sing a new song, saying, "Thou art worthy to take the book, and to open the seals thereof; for Thou wast slain, and hast redeemed us to God by Thy blood, out of every kindred, and tongue, and people, and nation, and hast made us unto our God kings and priests; and we shall reign on the earth." And every creature which is in heaven, and on the earth, and under the earth, and such as are in the sea, in millennial glory will sing, "Blessing, and honour, and glory, and power, be unto Him that sitteth upon the throne for ever and ever."

"Hallowed be Thy name!" "The name of the Lord is a strong tower, the righteous run into it, and are safe." What is in a name? Everything, revealing the unrevealed to darkened man; the photograph of the Eternal sent into time; earth's miniature of heaven's glory. While the Uncreated One has revealed Himself under many names, He has "in these last days spoken unto us by His Son, whom He hath appointed Heir of all things; by whom also He made the worlds, being the brightness of His glory, and the express image of His person." Only in Christ can we read the true name of God. We purpose to draw the attention of our readers to a few leading lines of study connected with "His name," and its bearing on us.

1. *Forgiveness.* 1 John ii. 12, "I write unto you, little children, because your sins are forgiven you for *His name's sake.*" The door of admission now for every child of Adam into the place of childhood of the Father, is the door of forgiveness. Education, moral culture, reformation, sanctification, are all taught inside, but the only door is forgiveness. That door has not been opened by our prayers, our tears, our groans, our works, or our feelings, but by His own hand, and for His name's sake. We did not draw to Him till He came to us. The debt was paid on Calvary's cross; the Resurrection is the Divinely-signed receipt for the abolished debt. "His name's sake" is the blank cheque handed down from, and signed by God Himself, to every sin-burdened soul, in which he can insert his own iniquity, transgression and sin. What is the value of a cheque on a bank? In itself only the value of the paper and the stamp upon it. But let a name be attached to it, and it then has all the value of the full resources of the one

who has signed it. All heaven's resources are opened to the sinner accepting His Divine cheque. Are the sins like scarlet? Is heaven not now the resting-place of Him whose blood can make the foulest clean, and for whose name's sake they shall be white as snow? Are they red like crimson, the damning colour of the hands of the murderer, red with the blood of a spotless victim? They shall be as wool, for forgiveness was preached first to Jerusalem murderers of the Prince of Life. Does the black indictment of Isaiah xliii. 23, 24, culminate in "Thou hast made me to serve with thy sins; thou hast wearied me with thine iniquities?" Are the resources of heaven available for this? Look at the hand of the holy God as He takes the blood of the Victim; listen to the words of the God of truth as He proclaims it to the most ungrateful of sinners: "I, even I, am He that blotteth out thy transgressions, for *Mine own name's sake*, and will not remember thy sins." Mark, it is not merely out of pity for us, far less on account of any external activity, self-righteous agility, or internal emotion on our part, but for *His own sake*. Glorious foundation; adamantine, everlasting, immovable rock, on which we build. In Him "we have redemption through His blood, the forgiveness of sins according to the riches of His grace."

2. *Guidance.* Psalm xxiii. 3, "He restoreth my soul: He leadeth me in the paths of righteousness for *His name's sake*." The justified man needs daily forgiveness. The quickened soul needs to be restored. The restored soul needs to be led, all has been anticipated and all has been met, because all is linked with His name, and "His name shall endure for ever; His name shall be continued as long as the sun." All within and around us is in constant change. Frames, feelings, fancies, tears, prayers, resolution, faith, hope, love, all have their ebbs and flows, but His name is "the same yesterday, to-day, and for ever." Has His blood been once presented at the throne for us, and accepted by us for justification before that throne? It is of continued and unceasing efficacy, and thus the blood of Jesus Christ is cleansing us (at every breath we breathe) from all sin. Am I prone to wander, prone to make mistakes, prone to follow the fleshly desires, prone to trip up and fall into the mire? "He restoreth my soul." Would it be a disgrace for me to dishonour my Saviour Redeemer, and cast a blot on that name I bear? "He leadeth me in the paths of righteousness for His

name's sake." His honour is compromised, and He is my guard-
ian Redeemer. He upholdeth my steps, because His name is
in them. On my eagle's wings, He has committed to me His
name. In my unwearied running, He has given me His name
to carry. In mine unfainting walk, His name supports me. In
the day of opposition, in my single-handed combat, when, having done all, I am now to stand, His name is shield, sword, and
helmet unto me; and in lying down in His green pastures, it is
His name which is my food. No turn of the way but is known
to Him. "Let him that nameth the name of Christ depart from
all iniquity." "He leadeth me for His name's sake."

3. *Communion.* Matt. xviii. 20, "Where two or three are
gathered together *in My name* there am I in the midst of them."
The forgiven and restored sinner is not condemned to tread a
solitary path, even though it lies through the wilderness. The
heaven-blessed soul is not called to partake of his joys alone.
He has even in the desert a fellowship of God with fellow-sin-
ners, saved by the same sovereign grace. He is to get sympathy
from, and to have sympathy with, others. Their numbers may
be very small—only two or three—but the communion is very
real. He requires no elaborate system of regulations, or code
of rules, to claim this Divine communion on earth. "His
name" is enough. The most elaborate and costly building that
an ordinary man may have built, is only the grand mansion or
castle of Mr. Great-purse; but a lowly cottage in which Her
Majesty resides becomes a palace. The most gorgeously
architectured building without God is a mere mass of building
material. But His name, with His first disciples at Jerusalem,
turned an upper ordinary family room into a heavenly temple, a
divine palace. The most eloquent preaching is but pleasing
talk springing from human brains, if "His name" is not its burden. The poorest elocutionist brimful of His name brings all
heaven before the eyes of those who have the spiritual faculty of
seeing. The most elaborate prayers may be but words of fancy,
feeling, or education, but "His name," breathed with stammer-
ing tongue, and from groaning heart, will open the windows of
heaven, sending down blessings, that we have not room enough
to receive. Magnificent music, splendid instruments, thorough-
trained singers, without "His name" as the centre of all their
praise, may command the applause of the ear, and
reach the rafters of the building, but they have nothing pleasing

to the ear of God; but in His name "we offer the sacrifice of praise continually, that is, the fruit of our lips giving thanks to His name." "Let us exalt *His name* TOGETHER."

4. *Activity.* 3 John 7, "For His name's sake they went forth, taking nothing of the Gentiles." Accepted according to the Victim's blood inside the veil, we are rejected with the Victim's flesh outside the camp. Our happy communion leads us to our living activity, dependent entirely on His name, independent of all the nations on the earth, their favours or frowns, their support or spite, their patronage or persecution. There is a fellowship through His name in this Divine activity on the earth. There is a giving and receiving. There is a Joshua wielding the sword, and a Moses on the hill-top with arms uplifted, and arms upheld by Aaron and Hur. "Beloved, thou doest faithfully whatsoever thou doest to the brethren, and to strangers, who have borne witness of thy love before the Church; whom, if thou bring forward on their journey after a godly sort, thou shalt do well; because that for His name's sake they went forth, taking nothing of the Gentiles. We, therefore, ought to receive such, that we might be fellow-helpers to the truth." This was written by an Apostle who knew much of His name, who in his younger days had lain on His bosom, and knew what it was to be independent of men, nature, or the world, and now in his old age puts himself alongside of the younger Gaius the well-beloved, encouraging him that "We might be fellow-helpers to the truth." The older and more experienced saint wrote this cheering word to the younger. Flattery is abominable, but cheering words to solitary labourers in the activity of their mission for His name, are as water in the dry desert. In works of faith, labours of love, and patience of hope, we are all prone to get disheartened. "His name" of good cheer warms us up again. So many mistakes, difficulties, worries, and disappointments lie in the path of the man who is endeavouring to live for His name alone, that there is not a Christian but occasionally needs a word of God-cheer to support him, and throw him on His name. Suspicions, insinuations, cold-shouldering, want of sympathy, malicious words, silent ignoring, are common enough. Let us imitate the more excellent way of John the aged, drawing close to his hundredth year, "that we may be fellow-helpers to the truth."

5. *Testimony.* Acts ii. 21, "Whosoever shall call on *the*

name of the Lord shall be saved." "The Lord said unto him (Ananias), Go thy way, for he (Paul) is a chosen vessel unto Me to bear *My name* before the Gentiles, and kings, and the children of Israel" (Acts ix. 15).

Peter was the Apostle to the circumcision, and he had to begin his testimony at Jerusalem, to be extended to Judæa, Samaria, and thence unto the uttermost part of the earth. Paul, on the other hand, was the Apostle to the Gentiles, and he was to testify inward towards the children of Israel. But the subject of each was the same. They were not left to choose their text. "The name of the Lord" was the salvation preached by Peter, the keynote of his testimony. "My name" was what Paul was to bear before Gentiles, kings, and Israel's children. Arts and sciences, politics and philosophy, earth's enactments or human cultus, were all secondary. "His name" was emblazoned on their banner, and under that flag they had the royal authority of Heaven to bear the testimony to every creature. We can sue for sufferance when we wish men to listen to our opinions, ideas, or thoughts, but with all the calm majesty and full Divine authority of our message, we can carry the standard that He gives us from palace to hovel, from frozen iceberg to coral strand, to barbarian, Scythian, black or white, bond or free, Jew or Gentile, and looking every fellow responsible being steadfastly in the face, can say on Heaven's authority, "If *thou* shalt confess with *thy* mouth the Lord Jesus, and shalt believe in *thine* heart that God hath raised Him from the dead, *thou* shalt be saved."

6. *Shame.* Acts v. 41, "And they departed from the presence of the council, rejoicing that they were counted worthy to suffer shame for *His name's sake*." This is the only crown that an unsympathetic world can give to those who bear His name in testimony. It is the crown of thorns in miniature—His suffering for righteousness at the hands of men. We can never touch His suffering at the hands of God for sin. And this shame carries with it a special blessing, because it is for His name it is obtained. Peter, who was foremost in bearing this shame for His name, writes more fully of it in his first letter, in the first chapter of which he tells us of the Old Testament Scriptures foretelling "the sufferings of Christ and the glory that should follow." In the second chapter, "This is thankworthy (or the character of grace), if a man for conscience toward God

endure grief, suffering wrongfully. For what glory is it if, when ye be buffeted for your faults, ye shall take it patiently? But if when ye do well and suffer for it, ye take it patiently, this is acceptable with God." Suffering as Christ suffered. "When He suffered He threatened not, but committed Himself to Him that judgeth righteously." In the third chapter, "If ye suffer for righteousness' sake, happy are ye; and be not afraid of their terror, neither be troubled." In the fourth chapter, "Rejoice, inasmuch as ye are partakers of Christ's sufferings. If ye be reproached for *the name* of Christ, happy are ye. If any man suffer as a Christian, let him not be ashamed, but let him glorify God on this behalf."

7. *Glory.* Rev. xxii. 4, "They shall see His face, and *His name* shall be on their foreheads." Soon the cross will give place to the crown, the curse from the earth will be removed, the glory will take the place of the shame, the forgiving and forgiveness having done their work for ever, the leading through the desert finished, the isolated gatherings now consolidated into one grand multitude—all nations now blessed in Him, and calling Him blessed, but still His name shall endure for ever. The outstanding feature of saintship will carry the impress of His name for ever. Angels may excel in strength and in wisdom, and may love to do His will; but the God and Father of our Lord Jesus Christ, revealed to us in Him who is the Lamb of God, taking away the world's sin, will be the name by which saints are known through the millennial age, and to the ages of ages, in that light which eclipses all human light of candle, or all natural light of the sun, for we shine in the light of God, and His name shall stamp each brow.

"They that know THY NAME will put their trust in Thee."

"HALLOWED BE THY NAME."

THE POWER OF GOD IN THE CHURCH.

" *That the righteousness of the law might be fulfilled in us, who walk not after the flesh, but after the Spirit. For they that are after the flesh do mind the things of the flesh; but they that are after the Spirit the things of the Spirit. For to be carnally minded is death; but to be spiritually minded is life and peace: Because the carnal mind is enmity against God; for it is not subject to the law of God, neither indeed can be."*—ROMANS viii. 4-7.

THE POWER OF GOD IN THE CHURCH.

THOSE to whom the Lord Jesus Christ gave power and authority were not privileged to be the instruments, by the Holy Ghost, of explaining that power to us. It was that Apostle who was saved by the risen Christ from the glory, the Apostle Paul, who has been privileged to put before us the source, the manifestation and the outflow of the power that is in Christ for His people. Such, I take it, is the meaning of the subject before us; it is power in the individual saints, and not so much power in the Church collective. We know very well that it is the Apostate Church that claims to be endowed with power as a Church. So in our subject it is, I believe, power in the individual saints of God that is meant—power in those who are united to the Lord Jesus Christ in the glory.

Now I wish to draw your attention to the teaching of the Apostle Paul concerning this power, and to his prayer concerning this power that is in Christ, for us who believe.

The first of these, his teachings as to the power, is given in Rom. viii., while his prayer is presented in Eph. i. and iii. His teachings you find in the middle of the three parts of Rom. viii. That chapter is very readily divided into three parts. The first closes at the tenth verse, the second at the thirtieth verse, and the third goes on to the end of the chapter. In the first we find what we are before God in Christ—"There is therefore now no condemnation to them that are in Christ Jesus." Our standing before God is given in contrast to what our standing was, as shown in Rom. v. As we were in Adam, so are we now in Christ. The second part gives us our present subject; not so much what we are in Christ, as what the Spirit of God is in us. And the last part gives us what God is for us

Now I intend to confine myself to a few thoughts from the Word, so that you may study them, with the aid of the Holy Spirit, for yourselves, and thus be taught of God.

In the first part of the chapter we have a new nature communicated to us, with new faculties. In the second part we have the Spirit of God with power, the Holy Ghost, the third Person of the blessed Trinity, given unto us. Not here is meant the new creation, which is sometimes called the spirit, but it is the Holy Ghost, the third Person of the Trinity, who is dwelling in us. In the last part we have God as our Protector—"If God be with us, who can be against us."

Notice that the mere possession of the new nature does not of itself imply that we have the power in us. Saved though we be, we are still dependent upon the Holy Ghost every moment for power, and it is not sufficient that we should be born again, we must have the power. There must be the living presence of the living Person to energize the new man, and the new creation. We are as dependent on the Spirit of God, moment by moment, for power, as we were when we first turned our dying eyes on the crucified Christ for salvation. This is God's great cure for Antinomianism—this inward power of the Holy Ghost. Not an *ab extra* power merely, but an *ab intra* power, controlled and guided by the power of God within us.

Now I will give you only a few watchwords from the eleventh verse onwards : "But if the Spirit of Him that raised up Jesus from the dead dwell in you, He that raised up Jesus from the dead, shall also quicken your mortal bodies, by His Spirit that dwelleth in you." The Holy Ghost is spoken of in this chapter under four names. He is called the "Spirit of God;" He is called the "Spirit of Christ;" He is called the "Spirit of Him that raised up Jesus from the dead;" and He is called the "Spirit that raised up Christ from the dead." In the ninth verse we have "The Spirit of God" as contrasted with the flesh: "Ye are not in the flesh, but in the Spirit, if so be that the Spirit of God dwell in you." Then as to our practical state we have "if any man have not the Spirit of Christ, He is none of His." Then he comes to the indwelling of the Spirit, he takes us from the humiliation of Jesus to the exaltation of Christ.

Now the first thing we learn is that He will quicken these mortal bodies of ours which attach us to the earth, and to the sins of this earth. Thus the Spirit is given us as a guarantee that our mortal bodies shall be quickened, and thus we know that by-and-by we shall reach the *terminus ad quem* when we reach the glory. Then our bodies shall be fashioned like unto His glorious body, not by any external force, but by His power dwelling in us. We shall not be dragged as felons before the bar of judgment, but by the power of the Holy Ghost dwelling in us, we shall be quickened whenever the Lord Himself shall come. It is worthy of remark that this indwelling of the Holy Spirit is passed over until the grand finale is introduced. It is the guarantee of the glory that is coming to Him, and to us. The guarantee that "when He shall appear we shall be like Him, for we shall see Him as He is, and every man that hath this hope in Him purifieth himself even as He is pure."

But till that glory is reached what is the power in us? The Apostle goes on very consistently, "Therefore brethren, we are debtors, not to the flesh, to live after the flesh. For if ye live after the flesh, ye shall die; but if ye through the Spirit do mortify the deeds of the body, ye shall live." The first thing, then, is resurrection, the next is mortification. Legalism would put mortification first, and then resurrection. But no, it is resurrection first, "If ye then be risen with Christ—mortify therefore your members, which are upon the earth."

So the second thought in connection with the indwelling of the Holy Spirit is this—that we are to mortify the deeds of the body, and those who are thus indwelt will still go forward, for it does not stop there, they will be led of the Spirit. "For as many as are led of the Spirit of God, they are the sons of God." We are not merely actually mortifying that which is evil, but actively pursuing that which is good, and that led by the Spirit of God. Thus mortification precedes leading. We are not, as some would have it, led and then mortified, but we are to mortify, and then be led. "For ye have not received the Spirit of bondage again to fear; but ye have received the Spirit of Son-standing, whereby we cry, Abba, Father!" "The Spirit of *Son-standing*," not merely children by adoption. Not simply as we might adopt a child, and then put him away when he comes of age, and fit to shift for himself, but sons by birth. There is a vague idea of that sort, but it is not found in Scripture. There we are shown to be sons by the new birth—we are born children of God, born again with the risen Christ. And thus we have the Son-standing by the Spirit dwelling in us—not the spirit of Sinai, not the spirit of the bond-woman, but the spirit of the free; and we cry "Abba, Father." Thus we reach the climax. Risen with Christ, mortifying the deeds of the flesh, led by the Spirit, by that heavenly, unnatural, unearthly, supernatural power we are guided and led through whatever maze this world may present. Then by this indwelling of the Holy Spirit we realize our Son-standing and cry "Abba, Father."

But further, "the Spirit Himself beareth witness with our spirit, that we are the children of God." The Spirit dwelling in us is a witness, not to our salvation, as is often said by mistake, but to our sonship. It is remarkable that there is no mention, made of the Holy Spirit in the Epistle to the Romans, (which is God's grand book for anxious inquirers,) until the man is taught to say that he is justified by faith, and has peace with God through our Lord Jesus Christ. Before that even the name of the Holy Spirit is never mentioned, as if He would not abstract the thoughts of the anxious inquirers from the grand point. But when the child is brought into the family, he learns the family secrets, and the family truths. He learns that he is no longer under the spirit of legalism, and that he is not expected to force himself to love God through fear, but rather he is to serve God through love, and that by the power of the Spirit dwelling within him, which shall lead him to rise instinctively to that higher motive of the new creation. He cries "Abba, Father," from no outward force compelling, but by an interior power witnessing with his spirit that he is the child of God.

But now we pass on to the next aspect of this indwelling of the Holy Spirit. We have seen the power of resurrection, the power for mortification, the power of guidance, the power of sonship, the power of hope, but now we have the power of sympathy. "Not only they, but ourselves also, which have the first-fruits of the Spirit, even we ourselves groan within ourselves, waiting for the adoption, to wit, the redemption of our body." Thus we have groanings in sympathy with the whole creation, and these groanings are produced by the Spirit of God. "For we are saved by hope, but hope that is seen is not hope; for what a man seeth, why doth he yet hope for?" And then in the 26th verse, "Likewise, the Spirit also helpeth our infirmities; for we know not what we should pray for as we ought; but the Spirit itself maketh intercession for us with groanings which cannot be uttered." We know not what we ought to pray for, but one thing we do know. And here I make a little variation in our translation. Verse 28, "*But*" (it should read *but*, not *and*) "we know that all things work together for good to them that love God." The contrast is here made with our ignorance; what we do not know is contrasted with what we do know. We do not even know how to pray aright, and what to pray for; and, we do not know how to speak, and we put the Word awkwardly before the people; but one thing we do know, and that is, that it will be well in the morning—yes, "we know that all things work together for good to them that love God." So then from the hope, the anticipation of the resurrection of the body, we have every gradation of His power till we reach the groaning in sympathy with the whole creation around us, and in sympathy with every part of our being; mental, moral, and physical groanings. So, while the material creation groans, the spiritual creation groans for the full manifestation of the sons of God. It groans, and is not yet satisfied; and rightly so, because it is the Holy Spirit that produces these groanings. Thus we have not merely the power of communion, the power of mortification, the power of guidance, the power of sonship, the power of witness, and the power of sympathy, but also the power of groaning within ourselves, for all that is abnormal in ourselves, and in the world around us, for all the evils, and wars, and woes, and miseries produced by sin; we sigh and groan for the time when we shall solve these mysteries. We do not want to be wise above what is written, but we find ourselves sighing and groaning in sympathy with the Holy Ghost, and by His power indwelling in us.

Then last of all, in the teaching of the Apostle, we find that by the power of the Spirit dwelling in us we arrive at the grand confidence amid all mutations and change. "If God be for us, who can be against us?"

Now we must pass on to the prayer of the Apostle Paul, in the Epistle to the Ephesians: "Blessed be the God and Father of our Lord Jesus Christ, who hath blessed us with all spiritual blessings in heavenly places in Christ." In Christ—all our well-springs are in Him, and all God's blessings for us are in Him. "According as He hath chosen us in Him before the foundation of the world, that we should be holy and without blame before Him in love." No one, even of the great angelic host, can stand before God without being holy, without blame and in love. So we, too, if we are to be before God, must be holy, must be without blame, and must be in love—holy in character, without blame in all our ways, and loving in our nature. When we find ourselves on earth—the very opposite of all this by nature unholy, full of blame, and loving ourselves and nothing else—well may we rejoice that in Him we have all we need, and in Him alone we are made presentable before God. In Christ we are made holy, in Him we are blameless, and in Him we learn to love.

Then, in connection with all this, the Apostle prays in the fifteenth and following verses, "Wherefore I also, after I heard of your faith in the Lord Jesus, and love unto the saints, cease not to give thanks for you, making mention of you in my prayers, that the God of our Lord Jesus Christ"—he does not bring in the title, "Father of our Lord Jesus Christ" here; that is in the third chapter, and opens up a wonderful domain of thought which we cannot now enter upon—"that the God of our Lord Jesus Christ, the Father of glory, may give unto you the spirit of wisdom and revelation, that the eyes of your understanding being enlightened." This is the Apostle's prayer for the saints; and we also pray that the eyes of our understanding may be enlightened, our eyes opened; so that we "may know what is the hope of His calling, and what the riches of the glory of His inheritance in the saints, and what is the exceeding greatness of His power to usward who believe." The Apostle prays that we may thus rise, to the hill-top, and that the mists and fogs may be taken from our eyes, so that we may see something of the wondrous extent of the inheritance gained for us. Here we have, as in other passages, word piled upon word, to enrich the teaching. We have here three distinct words in the Greek for *power*, each expressing a different shade of thought, and showing the power within us from our resurrection position. "The exceeding greatness of His power" (*dunamis*). "The working of His mighty power" (*kratos*). "Which He wrought in Christ when He raised Him from the dead, and set Him at His own right hand in the heavenly places, far above all principalities and power" (*exousia*). And you hath He quickened who were dead in trespasses and sins." For we must go on with that second chapter, for it follows from the resurrection power. May we go on to know more of this power, as those waiting for the manifestation of

Christ. Then, remember, we have to tell the world these things, and we have a wonderful message for any unconverted man here. We have to tell the good news, the glad tidings, the Gospel of God, which is the power of God unto salvation to every one that believeth.

One word more I must say ere I close. In the first chapter of Ephesians the Apostle prayed that we may know what we have got; but if we study the prayer of the third chapter we shall find there is something higher still. When you read it you find that there is something better than the knowledge of the glory, better than to know the possession we have got, and it is to "know the love of Christ which passeth knowledge," that love which was before the glory, that love which planned the glory; for the love that planned is higher and deeper than even the glory, so the Apostle bows his knee to the Father of our Lord Jesus Christ, that we may know that wondrous love.

One more solemn thought comes to me as we speak of this love, of this glory, of this eternity, and it is this: What is to be thy eternity, my friend? Men try to get quit of that thought of eternity, and try to blot out these two words, *eternity* and *punishment;* but put them out for a moment from Matt. xxv., and read the chapter without them. Is it not a solemn thought even yet? "These shall go away"—stop there if you will. Away—*away*—where? The sweetest word uttered by Christ to poor man is, *Come !* To the weary soul He says, "Come unto Me"; and to those on His right hand, "Come, ye blessed." But away, away!—may those awful words never be heard by any here. God grant it may not be. "These shall go away." Away from Christ, away from God, away from life, away from love; away from His tears, His cross, His power, His glory, and His Spirit. Away, away! Is the word for you to be *away*, or *come?* Now He has opened your way to the glory and pleads with you to come!

THE FULNESS OF BLESSING.

"*Blessed be the God and Father of our Lord Jesus Christ, who hath blessed us with all spiritual blessings in heavenly places in Christ.*"—EPHESIANS I. 3.

THE FULNESS OF BLESSING.

THE first chapter of the Epistle of Paul to the Ephesians, 3d verse, says—"Blessed be the God and Father of our Lord Jesus Christ, who hath blessed us with all spiritual blessings in heavenly places in Christ." This seems to be the fulness of blessing, and to tell us in whom it is provided. "Blessed be the God and Father of our Lord Jesus Christ, who hath blessed us with all spiritual blessings in heavenly places in Christ." It seems also to draw before our eyes a contrast with former blessing that the great Creator, Jehovah had given to Israel in the days of Israel's glory. The basket and the store being full, we have evidences of righteousness and righteous living. That they should dwell in the land, and have food, was the great promise given to Israel. They were blessed with all temporal blessings in earthly places—in Canaan. Their blessings were earthly and temporal, and their sphere was Canaan. But now, since the Christian dispensation has dawned, and since in Christ Jesus there is neither male nor female, Jew nor Gentile, barbarian, Scythian, bond or free, our sphere is changed, our position is changed; we are blessed with all spiritual blessings. The heavenly places, and He in whom is found blessing, is Christ. "Hath blessed us." It doesn't say "shall bless us," or "is about to bless us." It is "hath blessed us." There is not a single Christian, a single believer in the Lord Jesus Christ, but has all blessing. There has always been a tendency in all ages among all men, among all minds, to make distinctions between genuine Christians. Laity and clergy have no foundation in the Word of God. There is no such thing. We have pastors, teachers, evangelists. There is no inner circle—a chosen lot that comes nearer to

God. He has blessed us with all spiritual blessings. The Church of Rome has introduced all these things, making it appear that one Christian has more favour in the Church of God than another. There is no such thing as mediatorial priesthood, one Christian for another. We are all priests unto God. "He hath made us unto our God kings and priests." We have all an equal right of drawing near. There is no selection of some people as having got the blessing. There is no blessing that we can have, but God has already given us in Christ; though, alas! there are many blessings we have received that we never think of. There is no blessing—let it be called the fulness of blessing, let it be called any sphere of blessing—there is no blessing that you require, or your heart can think of, that we have not already in Christ.

Fellow-believer in the Lord Jesus Christ, there are many blessings in Christ that we never think of, and we don't know of. And it is on this account, among others, that we try and stir one another up to know what blessing is —to know of whom to be got, to know how it is to be appropriated, to know how it is to be communicated. The youngest child of God, the youngest convert to the Lord Jesus, has a whole Christ, and nothing else, and the most aged saint, having the greatest experience, has a whole Christ, and nothing more. We need the experience of the blessing as granted by the God and Father of our Lord Jesus Christ in the gifts, or the gift of His Gift of Gifts—all other gifts in one—Christ. I might illustrate this subject, by saying that the gift He gives us is like a large casket full of choice jewels. He gives us a casket, and in it all the jewels. At first we only find the necessary provision for our daily use. The first thing that we rejoice in is in the anthem. We read of it in the 5th chapter to the Romans— "Being justified by faith, we have peace with God through our Lord Jesus Christ." We are too prone to look at what we have done ourselves, the sins we have actually committed; but the first thing we find is peace. The young convert comes to find that not only does he need peace, not only was he guilty of what he had done, but that he produced sin. Not only had he something against him, but something within him. He looks into the casket. He needs no new casket. He has only to unfold what he has already received. After a time he finds that he requires more, so he goes on to the 8th of Romans, and sees he is standing in a new man. His sins are blotted away, and the righteousness of God's law fulfilled. Now he sees some of the preciousness of the casket, and he sings the anthem of the 8th chapter of Romans—"There is therefore now no condemnation." Not only, I am not condemned, but there is no condemnation for me.

Thus we have the second stage in the examination of the ripe, full blessing we have received. We have got past the initial stages—got past the idea of condemnation, and have found out that by the righteousness and blessing of God, there is no condemnation. But we require to learn more. We are taken away to the desert of loneliness, we are taken away to adversity, to sadness and sorrow, to the toils of every-day life. We don't need to apply for a new casket of blessing. We have only to come to the old one that we already have. We have all in Him—in Christ. We don't go to receive a new Christ. Do I get weary and retire to a corner of the desert? I find in Him my food still. Do I get to some bleak, barren desert, and find that I am thirsty? I find that He is the water of refreshment. Do I get into some benighted part, and see no opening out? He is a pillar to guide me by night, and a cloud to shelter me by day. And thus I find another layer of blessed gems of glorious perfection, and the more experience I get, the more I know of these jewels. Thank God for experience!

Young Christians know little about Christ. It may be, as often as not, that they use their strength pretty freely. There is progress in all Christian life, and in all Christian knowledge, and it is a remarkable thing that the progress in the experience, is quite different from what we would expect. We all renew our strength; but how do we renew it? The first thing we do in renewing our strength is to mount up on wings like eagles. They fly. You would think that that was a fair development of strength, whereas it is only the first manifestation of it. You will generally find young converts practising this. Let them. We have all to sink soon enough. Why, I have seen scores of young converts who thought that they would never tread the earth again, never see a bit of mud all the rest of their life, never do anything wrong. Let them have it, dear fellow-believer. Let us all have wings if we can. We may be all the better for a little Christian gymnastics. We don't fly long.

We soon come back to the earth. The next stage in advancement is to run and not be weary. It is a long race, and a hard race, and a difficult race, and we have to lay aside every weight. What do you know about running? There is a day coming when you will have to walk—to walk and not to faint in that narrow path, in the footsteps of that One in whom I am blessed.

There are days of fainting as well as flying. There are days when fainting fits come on. But we have not only to walk, we have to stand—a different experience from flying. The evidence of blessing we had in the flying will not do for the standing. We must go back to the casket—to the store-house —but still God hath blessed us with all spiritual blessings. "And having done all, to stand." As Martin Luther, the grand reformer, said, when told that all the world was against him, "Well, I'm against all the world." He knew the grace that could be found in the fulness of blessing. Anything more? O yes. We have another stage yet. After we have done all, and got the blessings to know what to do in standing —"He maketh me to lie down in green pastures," but it is the perfect repose of his own provision.

In whom is it provided? It is in the God and Father of our Lord Jesus Christ. I have given you some specimens in one line of action. Israel got their blessings from the Creator and Jehovah; our peculiar blessings are from the God and Father of our Lord Jesus Christ. This is why the blessings are spiritual, the blessings are in heavenly places, and the blessings are in Christ. The next two verses, the 4th and 5th, throw some light on these two relations. In the 4th verse it is in connection with Him as God, in the 5th verse as Father; in the 4th verse, he sees the necessity of God's nature, that we "be holy and without blame before Him;" in the 5th verse the purposes of His love, "Children to Himself."

Any being to live before Him must be "without blame, holy, and in love." How can we ever have such blessing in which to stand "before Him?" He chose us "in Him before the foundation of the world," and therefore nothing can alter this, because it was before time, before man was created.

The prayer in the first chapter is to the *God* of our Lord Jesus Christ that He may give us the spirit of wisdom and revelation that we may know what we have. In the third chapter there is quite a different prayer, to the *Father* of our

Lord Jesus Christ, that we may know the love of Christ, which passeth knowledge."

In the present day there is much sentimental talk about the Fatherhood of God; I should like to hear a great deal more about the Godhood of God. "The world's universal Father!" There is no such thing in all Scripture. He may be talked of in the way of Father, as He is our Maker, and we His offspring. A carpenter could be called the father of a chair. Read from the 15th verse of this 1st chapter of Ephesians, and you have there the most remarkable prayer in the whole Bible. Mark you, there is not a single word about love, or kindness, or peace, or mercy. The holy God must have holy creatures before Him. All who stand before Him must have this characteristic—angels, principalities, and powers. The necessity of His nature requires it. But how can we stand before Him blameless, and in love? I know that I am blameworthy, and I know I have that within my heart which is not love. But He chose us in Him before the foundation of the world. The question has been settled. The arrangement was before time and man, and cannot be altered by time. Some men talk about the gifts, the atonement, justification, as just little somethings which God has given. Some have a limited atonement, and some a universal. We come to Christ, and get the atonement in Him. You would think that there were only scattered bits of atonement flying about for a few people to appropriate. There is Christ. I come to Him—to the holiness, to the blamelessness, to the love God has seen in Him, and the Father has ordained in Him, before the foundation of the world; and there I get life. In Him I get all the righteousness of God, and the holiness of God. That is the meaning of standing before Him in holiness, and blamelessness, and in love. He must be God; He may be Father. In all circumstances the necessities of His nature must be met. It is quite a mistake to sing, "I wish I were an angel." We have a far better and higher blessing than an angel. You are made priests to God. God was never manifested in the nature of angels. He took not upon Him the form of principalities. He became Man. And this Man holds the sceptre of the universe in His hands. Oh, brethren, let us rise up to the dignity of our sonship, and dare to be like Him, dare to live up to Him. He has the fulness of blessing. He wanted some "to Himself"—not merely to stand before

Him; He has angels who serve Him day and night. But He has given us Christ, who is the fulness of blessing. Let us get to the top of this Ben Nevis of blessing. Look above you, look up the empyrean. He has given you gifts and blessings. The blessings are there for us to appropriate as we need them. We have a full Christ; in Him we see our God, in Him we see our Father. Open your eyes to see what you have; it is all your own, given by the God of glory. But remember there is something before the gifts. Remember the Blesser. I fear there is a danger in being taken up with the blessings instead of the Blesser. Let us rejoice in the blessings that Christ has given us, and let us also rejoice in the grace that has given us the blessing.

THE PRACTICAL ASPECTS OF THE HOPE.

" Beloved, now are we the sons of God ; and it doth not yet appear what we shall be : but we know that, when He shall appear, we shall be like Him ; for we shall see Him as He is. And every man that hath this hope in Him purifieth himself, even as He is pure."—I JOHN III. 2, 3.

THE PRACTICAL ASPECTS OF THE HOPE.

THE study of prophecy is not the hope of the Church. It is exceedingly interesting, full of interest at every point, every chapter, every verse, every word, but the study of prophecy is not the hope of the Church, and my subject is "The practical aspects of this Hope." The hope of the Church is something more tangible, and more sweet. It is a living Person, and His return. It is the return of our blessed Lord, and not the details of prophetical truth, either enunciated in the Old or New Testament, or fulfilled in detail, but the return of a person, so that while some might think, "I have not the knowledge, I have not the Hebrew, I have not the Greek, and I lack many other qualifications to follow all these distinctions"—my friends all I want to ask of you, is this, Have you a heart for the return of our blessed Lord? It is the heart for Him that is the great hope of the Church of the living God. And my text has been largely painted for me for this occasion. I do not ask you to look at your Bibles, because the painter has been very kind, and painted it in full blaze before you. My text you will find in the words,—"SURELY I COME QUICKLY." This is from the heart of the Bridegroom. "Surely I come quickly,"—and a couple of millenniums is quickly in His mind. "I come quickly"—for the desire to return, oversteps all millenniums—"Behold, I come quickly." Then we have the response in the next place, the response of the Bride, which echoes back and says, "Amen, even so come, Lord Jesus." We are not to be behindhand in the response of love, because it is the same Spirit that energizes us in measure, that fills Him without measure; and so the challenge of love, "Surely, I come quickly," is met with the response of love, "Amen, even so come, Lord

Jesus." It limits all those hundreds of years, and seals, and vials, and everything else, because the nearest point to a benighted traveller on a dark night, is the light-house. He sees nothing between. "Amen, even so come Lord Jesus." Then the practical application of the hope, "Let your loins be girded about, and your lamps burning." I am thankful my text is so patent, that we have not to look down, but we have all to look up, and I trust we will all be looking up, and in that attitude be knowing the aspects of the blessed truth. "Let your loins be girded about, and your lights burning." It concludes all—fitly chosen and well put. It includes all that we ought to be and all that we ought to do. We ought to be as men, whose loins are girded, not in confusion and disorder, but tucked up for the fight and ready for anything, ready as men of war, not as men going to sleep, but as men who are putting on the armour of good soldiers and not sleepers, with loins girt about with truth, and then what we ought to be doing, just letting our light shine, because in the midnight darkness we are waiting for God's Son from heaven. I remember the time—and you will pardon personal reminiscences—when I am sure, though I was a Christian, I did not realize the least about girding up the loins and tucking them about with the girdle of truth. All the garments were in the mud. When one tried to run, one tripped, because of the long flowing Eastern robe. You cannot run unless you are made snug and ready for a race, or a battle. I know myself, that while I merely stood on the grand, glorious central truth of salvation from sin, it was as though the battle had not been completely won. In my own experience I tried to think, that when you get one foot down on the cross, you are there secure, but that did not feel so strong, till I got the other on the crown, and there a man can stand, and having done all to stand, in the evil day, with cross and crown as the grand groundwork on which He stands.

"Let your loins be girded about, and let your lights shine in this world." "Ye are the salt of the earth : ye are the light of the world." It is "Let your light shine." It is not by any forced sort of artificial method by which we pump up oil or make great spurts, or make large fireworks on great occasions. There are some firework Christians. They seem by some incidental accident to blaze up occasionally, and then they relapse into a quiescent state, waiting for some other blazing time, when they can make some further wonderful demonstration, and do something great.   That is not the testimony of our blessed Lord. I believe that we all have need of patience—a patient continuance in well-doing ; and if you look at the Lord's coming, you will find it often mixed up, and connected with patience.   "Be patient for the day of the Lord is at hand."   Sometimes district-visitors in a little corner of God's vineyard, get paralyzed in their action, and they think, "If I could only preach to twenty or more old women I should do very well, but I have not the gift of utterance ;" and instead of going the round of their little beat, bearing a glorious testimony, and with their light shining to His dear people, they get disheartened.   " Let patience have her perfect work."   Ye have need for patience.   It is by patient continuance in well-doing that we are to reap the glory of im-mortality.   I was asked if it was not a great thing to be able to preach to a lot of people.   I said, " Whether it is or is not, the Lord tells us that true religion does not consist in that at all.   He tells us that true religion consists in visiting the fatherless and widows, and we can all do that."   It is not some great work, some spasmodic effort, some great throwing off of scintillas of light on occasional opportunities, but it is by that constant living in communion with an absent one, filled with His oil, and showing forth His light, that we fulfil the text, " Let your lights be burning."   If you look through the Word of God you will find that there is scarcely a subject, scarcely a practical subject connected with Christianity, but is linked with the coming of the Lord.   Holiness—that deepest of all subjects to us : " Beloved now are we the sons of God, and it doth not yet appear what we shall be ; but we know that, when He shall appear, we shall be like Him ; for we shall see Him as He is. And every man that hath this hope in Him purifieth himself, even as He is pure."   Every one that hath the hope, this hope of being with Him, and being like Him, His own being with Him, and His own being like Him, " purifieth himself even as He is pure."   His own heart goes out towards us, and says, " What I say to you, I say unto all, Watch."   It takes us in-to the line of watchfulness.   I know well when I am a few days away from home, the longer I am away, the more my little boys are watching for my return.   I say to them, I will be back such and such a time, and there is not a cab that comes to our door but what they say, " This is father now " and why ? because they have got all the little things that I would like, put out for me.   If they have been into my study scattering things, all the papers are put right and tidy, because they know I am coming quickly and soon.   They are watching.   They have, perhaps, got a little flowerpot with a flower in it stuck on my study table, and they want to make it nice, and beautiful, and happy against my return.   They know that their father is coming.   They are watching for him, and waiting.

Talking about prophetical questions, and knowing about these most interesting things, which we sometimes would have a great delight to go into (I do not say always to agree upon), is very interesting ; and I think we have a considerable amount to say in a difference.   However, all is apart from the blessed hope of watching for a glorious Person Himself, to come at any moment, and nothing between Himself and me—waiting for Him to return to-night.   A friend said to me the other day, "Was not Paul waiting for Him?"   "Certainly ; and that is why I am, because I find Paul was so anxiously waiting."   "Then," he said, "is not Paul disappointed?"   "Disappointed!" I said, "How can Paul be disappointed?   Is it a disappointment to go up and be waiting in the beautiful drawing-room, rather than in the dark, dingy apartment where we are waiting for Him now?   I should think he is a little more comfortable where he is, but he is waiting for the same thing now, as he was upon the earth.   First of all, it is much nicer in the drawing-room than down in the dungeon.   'I have a desire to depart, and to be with Christ, which is far better.'   But show me that by departing, and being with Christ, he is not waiting for the same blessed hope as you and I are waiting for here, and "the appearing of His glory."   It is not so much the glorious appearing ; it is the appearing of the glory of our great God and Saviour Jesus Christ.   Not only you and I are panting and saying, "Lord Jesus come ;" and not only the Apostle Paul and all the sainted ones, I believe, from Abel downwards, are saying, "Lord Jesus come ;" but I believe that, better than you waiting, and better than Paul waiting, is this, that the Lord Jesus Christ Himself is waiting for the blessed day.   The saints in the disembodied state, and the saints upon the earth are waiting ; but, brighter and brighter than all, the Saviour in the glory is waiting patiently till His enemies are put under His feet to stand upon, when He shall take to Himself His great power, and reign.

.Are we asked to sit down in fellowship, and show the Lord's death? What is it that our eyes are lifted up to? "To show the Lord's death till He come." It is the one visible link between the two advents of our Lord, that blessed supper that He originated. The one visible link is the breaking of the bread and the tasting of the wine, between the death of Christ on Calvary, and the crowning glory that is to fill the whole world. Are we in sorrow? Have we lost loving ones? "The Lord Himself shall descend from Heaven with a shout, with the voice of the archangel, and with the trump of God: and the dead in Christ shall rise first. Then we which are alive and remain, shall be caught up together with them in the clouds, to meet the Lord in the air: and so shall we ever be with the Lord. Wherefore comfort one another with these words." It is not "now they have died, they have gone from us, and they will not return to us." That is not our hope; but "we wish you quickly back for us, for the Lord shall descend with you for us." You have to comfort one another with *these words*, that the dead in Christ shall rise first, and we who are alive and remain shall be caught up.

Then as for Israel, poor, broken, defeated, scattered, rebellious, unbelieving Israel, driven to the winds of heaven, has the Lord no eye for thee? Ah, yes; we know it, and we know that He is looking for them in all parts of the earth; and Israel will be gathered again, and will be united, and will stand together in the house of the Lord. And then will come the day when Ephraim shall no longer envy Judah, nor Judah vex Ephraim. They will stand together, and sing the grand fraternal Psalm, "Behold how good a thing it is for brethren to dwell together in unity!"

Whatever we look at around us, or within us, we have the solution to all our difficulties in that glorious fact that our Lord is to return, and that right is to take the place of wrong, and that the Prince of Peace is to take the throne usurped by him who is the prince of the power of the air.

I must confess my words on a subject that eternity will unfold must be weak; but every kind of Christian, whatever he may be, is cheered up, and is comforted, and is stimulated by this blessed hope. And as for its being practical, tell me one truth more practical. Certainly we have one truth more precious, we must say; for the cross can never cease to be the most

precious truth, as on it depends our peace for time and eternity.
The cross! oh, let us never forget it! The cross! the most
mighty centre that ever the universe of God, or the eternity of
God, heard of or saw, where God has been glorified, and His
law magnified, and His name honored, and His righteousness
vindicated, and His holiness seen, when He could by no means
clear His own Son when sin was upon Him; and where the
poor sinner can see the hatefulness of his sin, and the love of
his Saviour-God.   Oh, it is the cross!

> "The cross, the cross! the Christian's only glory;
>   I see the standard rise!
> Sing on, sing on, the cross of Christ before thee!
>   That cross all hell defies!"

But when we have rejoiced our spirits with the life that is in
the look—

> "There is life in a look at the crucified One"—

then what, as Christians, are we to get? Why, the very next
truth, with nothing between, which is the crown of our blessed
Lord.   It is the sufferings of Christ, and the glory of Christ,
that shall be revealed.   There is no gulf between, in His mind;
and if He in His own love and wondrous wisdom has made a
pause between the two, that He might show the wonders of His
grace, in gathering together one new man, out of Jew and Gentile, and to show the power of a resurrection life, and a resurrection bride, shall I not enter into His view, into His idea, into
His glorious hope, of the return of my Master, and the appearance of His crown upon the earth?

If I am a sufferer, if I am a soldier, or if I am a student, this
blessed Book is altogether, and at all times, and only practical
in its bearing from God to me.   If I am a sufferer, the aching
head shall soon be decked with the crown of gold; the weary
feet shall soon walk in the streets of the golden city.   Sufferer,
lift up thy head!   Weary one, thy Lord is coming!   Thou
mayest not have to face death at all.   There is no certainty.
A Christian that says, "I shall not die," is very foolish; a
Christian that says, "I must die," is very ignorant; so between
the two we take whatever the Lord sends first.   We have no
voice in the matter; we take what He sends.   And so the suffering one sees the Lord coming for Him, to reveal all the glory
of His name.

Fighting one ! soldier ! servant ! stand fast ; "hold fast that thou hast ; let no man take thy crown." Our salvation is nearer than when we believed. Do not be wishing to do some great thing, like Naaman, but go ye and do your little things faithfully. You do not know what it is to be in the true "King's" college. This is the "King's" college, where we are all being trained for kings. When a captain of a vessel has some important thing to do, he does not send the youngest apprentice to do it. If it is to hold a rope, the letting go or holding fast of which may entail the safety or capsizing of the vessel, he sends the old grim veteran that can stand, and knows nothing but to obey, "Now," he says, "hold fast the rope !" and there the old weather-beaten tar will hold. Suppose some friend comes, and says, "Tom, what are you holding on to that rope for—it goes through a hole, and we can't see where it is going, or know what it is doing ?" "Get out of my way ; let me hold on here !" "But you should see what you are doing, and see the results." "Go away, and mind your business," would reply the weather-beaten tar, if, indeed, he deigned to reply at all. Or perhaps he would be asked, "Why are you holding on there ?" "Because Captain told me ; that is enough for me." And the captain knows well who will stand by him, and who he can put to the execution of a difficult enterprise. It is the man who will obey without asking any questions ; and so in the glory that is to come, I believe our Lord will know who He can depend upon, and who knows how to obey without asking any questions, and what is meant by "Well done, good and faithful servant !"

Are you a student of God's blessed word ? Are you desirous to know His mind ? Then look at the Lord's coming back again, as the solution of all your difficulties. Do you say, the love of many is waxing cold ? My friend, is not that the fulfilment of the Master's word ? Do you find the whole of Christendom being leavened ? Is not that the Master's word ? Would it not have been very strange if it had not come true ? Is it not the solution of all your difficulties ? Instead of sitting at home, and wondering how God could permit such things, rise up in the dignity of intelligence, in His own mind, and go forth to do His work, daring to do for Him, knowing He has the whole of the responsibility in His hand. This is the practical aspect.

I was told, but it was many years ago, that such a blessed hope would stultify missionary effort. I deny it; emphatically I deny it. It is the very opposite. I believe that this hope, that this one mainspring of thought, ought to lead us to evangelize the world. I believe that the great, grand, criminal mistake of our dispensation has been (and especially of our land at this moment), that we have been trying with a false idea to convert patches, instead of to evangelize the world. " Go ye into all the world," is the command ; and what do we find ? You keep thirty thousand men, as it were, on the point of your finger, and all the rest is dark. Thirty thousand ministers and preachers in Great Britain, and four hundred millions in China who never heard the Gospel, because we have been trying to convert Great Britain, and not to evangelize China and Japan. It is because we have been disobedient that we have met with so little success. Suppose every minister of every church and denomination in this land were swept away to China and Japan to the glory of God, and that twenty-five or twenty-eight peripatetic evangelists were left at home, to go through England and Scotland, and give an occasional day's preaching in London, Liverpool, Hull, and Edinburgh ; then you would about equalize what heathenism is just now. It is disobedience ; and I confess to my belief that part of the penalty for it is, that we have not been seeing what this dispensation exists for—to gather out a people for His name who shall be unto Himself, gathered out of every kingdom, and nation, and tongue. If the state of the church is thus made plainly seen, and the responsibilities of the saints made sure and fast by that blessed hope, what about the world that we are in ? Just the same. Congresses may meet, and God grant that peace may follow ; but though statesmen may seem bewildered, and the greatest in the earth may stand appalled, the Christian, with that blessed hope, stands calm ; whatever the notions about the seven seals may be, whatever his idea of progressive, or historical, or futurist notions may be, he stands calm. " He that believeth shall not make haste." We pray for peace, and, blessed be God, He has told us to do so. We pray that we may have peace in our times ; but whatever comes amid the overturning of nations, and the wreck of kingdoms, the Christian is calm—calm amid war, or famine, or pestilence, or sword, or destruction, or nakedness, knowing that in all these things we "are more than conquerors." As patiently waiting for God's Son from heaven, who, instead of the congresses that men can gather, and the scheming of worldly politicians, will return to put down all rule and all authority, and to break principalities and powers, and let the peers of glory see what government is upon this world; when He shall come down to make all wrongs right, to chain the prince of darkness, and to reign before His ancients gloriously.

MISCELLANEOUS.

"SAY NOT IN THINE HEART."

ROMANS x. 6.

MAN always begins to suggest the remedy for himself: God has expected that man will say something in his heart, so He advises him not to do it.

"Say not in thine heart,"—for this is the one thing man begins to do, to guess, to say "Peradventure, perhaps," and "I hope so." "Say not in thine heart." You and I have to meet God whether we wish it, or like it, or not, how long soever we may put it off (for we have the fatal freedom to put it off); it is coming, we must meet the God with whom we have to do; there is a hereafter, and you and I have to be in it; and our condition in that hereafter is to be fixed now, and you and I have something to do with the conditions which fix that state, therefore, "say not in thine heart."

This is what the righteousness of faith speaketh with authority. As an oracle from God it comes, asking you and me to hear because it speaks.

I. It speaks to us negatively, it tells us what *not* to do.

II. It speaks to us positively, it tells us what to do.

The preceding verse tells us that "Moses describeth the righteousness which is of the law, that the man which doeth these things shall live by them." No man ever did them, so no man ever lived by them, and Moses does not describe the *man*, but the "righteousness of the law which saith," an idea which has never had a tangible reality. The word which the Divine writer has chosen is "describeth," painteth—the righteousness of the law, but the righteousness of faith comes, speaking and asking us to believe. No man ever kept the law, so no man ever lived by it, but the righteousness of faith comes speaking on this wise,

"Say not in thine heart." Most people anxious about their salvation are communing with their own hearts, and not listening to the conditions which God lays down.

A young man once entered my room, and paused some time before he spoke. At last he said he had applied to several people, but all had passed him on to some one else, saying it was not their business. He said, "I have read several religious books, yours among the rest, and I want to know how to get my soul saved."

I replied, "I will not pass you on, for it is my business to heal you if I can. What is your disease?" He hesitated, so I said, "You cannot feel as you would like to do, is that it?" "Yes, that is it, I cannot feel right." I said, "You have to do with the just and holy God, who will never change His laws for us, a God of infinite majesty, and you begin to talk of your *feelings;* would it not be better to find out the conditions He has laid down?"

"If you owed £100 would it not be better to try and work with your hands to pay it off, than to talk of how you *feel* about your debt; or suppose I appoint you by letter to come to my house at twelve to-morrow. You come, and are told that I have been out for half an hour, and shall not return for two hours. When I see you, I say, 'Oh, I felt you would not come.' You show me my own letter, and say, 'You appointed me to come at twelve.' We have nothing to do with the feelings; we have to do with the Book, and what God says in it. It is not my feelings or yours. What is the use of that when there are conditions laid down?"

Submission is the point, not the details so much, not the clearness of conception, as the submission to the dictates of another, so the longing soul will be satisfied. I believe no one went to hell who longed for Christ. The devil would say, "Get away, we have no room for Christ here." I said to the young man, "Will you submit? it is all laid down here, you have only to endorse the cheque, we have it here payable to sinner, or bearer, a blank cheque signed and sealed in blood, and any man can lift it up out of this verse I am reading, he can endorse it on the back, and it is payable on demand." He saw he had to look away from himself to what had been done by another, that God was pleased to say He was satisfied with the work done on Calvary's Cross, and if He is pleased, I may be thankful to accept it. I think the young man went away, rejoicing in Christ's finished work. If I could have a trumpet tongue which would sound from one end of Britain to the other, there is one thing I should like to say to one class of people ; not to Christians, for they have got to the root of the matter, and they will, "some on boards and some on broken pieces of the ship," all get safe to land; not to the godless, for they do not care, and I may not have capacity to reach them ; but to a large class, a middle class, not careless nor doubting, not running to excess of rioting, but not standing on the rock ; and the text I would preach from to them would be, "Say not in thine heart," go not by what thy heart says. To turn men in to what they feel, instead of out to what God has done and said, is the crying heresy of the present day, and this is our mission—to come with the oracles of God as contrasted with feelings. "Say not in thine heart," because all men are ready to go by what they feel, and three quarters of evangelical preaching is founded upon this sensational religion, "Do you feel God's Spirit working within you ? Do you feel getting better ?—then go on and get to heaven." Many good men have said it, but it is not in my Bible, from Genesis to Revelation. I have searched from board to board, and the word feeling in connection with salvation, is not to be found in it. I believe it has been got from the devil. The adversary of souls goes with the preacher, night after night, and does all he can to thwart the Word ; he comes as an angel of light, not as the serpent, for then you would not listen to him; he comes neither outwardly immoral, nor outwardly out and out for Christ. If he came as a liar, you would say, "Get thee behind me, Satan ;" if he came and said the Bible was not true, and there was no hell, and no heaven, you would say, "Get thee behind me, Satan ;" all these are lies, and you would find them out soon ; so he will not do this with you who are better taught, but he will come as an angel of light ; or if he sees you inclined to one line of things, he will give you what will please you, lest you should hear and be saved. Our whole powers are devoted week after week to get people saved ; his whole work is to blind people, for, "if our gospel be hid, it is hid to them that are lost, in whom the God of this world hath blinded the minds of them which believe not, lest the light of the glorious gospel of Christ, who is the image of God, should shine unto them." What a diabolical work, to keep people unsaved, like those wreckers that rear the beacon-light on the iron-bound shore, that the sailor may be dashed to pieces, even so he rears a beacon-light, but it leads to death, ruin and desolation.

Satan has substituted two things for the gospel which "is the power of God." To those who have a traditional Christianity, he finds he must do other things than contradict the Bible ; so he comes and substitutes one truth for another, and there are two great lines of truth which he has taken and put in the place of one and the same truth. The one is the *life* of Christ ; this was one great thing I was taught in early life, and my idea was that in order to be saved I must live a life like His ; children are taught this still, for the devil has taken that grand truth that we should *imitate* the life of Christ, and he has put it in the place of Calvary and Golgotha, and the dying Lamb of God. We need not begin with Christ at Bethlehem, He began with us there, we begin with His death, and having secured His death we go back, and retrace the steps of His life. I believe Satan has invented no greater error than that of substituting the life of Christ for His death. The Apostle Paul says, "God forbid that I should glory save in the *cross* of our Lord Jesus Christ," not the *manger*.

"PEACE ON EARTH."

LUKE ii. 14.

THE Crimean War, the Franco-Germanic War, the Turko-Russian War, are all fresh in the memories of this generation. Has there ever been universal peace in this world since the days of Christ? Professor Tyndall wishes to explain the anthem of the angels, when they sing of, "Peace on Earth," as being merely the dramatic representation of the devout wishes of men; because, he thinks, that if it were a real anthem struck by superhuman beings as the key-note of the result of the visit of the Prince of Peace, history has proved that it was a mistake. Scientific men are to be carefully listened to when they are in their own department; but they make sad havoc when they enter into another room of God's great universe. On bones, muscles, nerves, cerebellum and brain, the information they give is most exact, and, therefore, interesting; but when with scalpel, microscopes and mere scientific method, they enter the domain of revelation, theology or exegesis, they are as miserably adrift as a blacksmith with his tools would be, entering a watchmaker's workshop; the anatomy of the human body is perfect; the anthem of the angelic host is perfect; but anatomy does not explain anthem, as anthem does not disturb anatomy.

Nothing could be more perfect, comprehensive and extensive, than that beautiful *Gloria in Excelsis*.

1. "Glory to God in the highest." The whole universe must re-echo this note. Not a sun, nor planet, nor comet, nor system, but sounds back this strain. Mountain, rock, river and ocean, peal forth its music. Forest and field, and everything that hath breath adds, Amen. And first above and beyond all things, for which Christ came, was to show glory to

God in the highest, infinitely beyond man's interests, or thoughts, hopes, or fears. But we descend from the generic song of all the universe to the specific note for earth.

2. "Peace on earth." We know the desolation of war, the absurdity of war, the unreasonableness of war, the inhumanity of war, the ungodliness of war. We have yet to learn the supreme, God-like blessings of peace on earth. Professor Tyndall finds difficulty here; we can see none. Professor Tyndall proposes to deliver a lecture. Let us suppose that on arriving at the place announced he was arrested and put into prison on a charge of treason. Does Professor Tyndall not see that his lecture must be postponed? The path of the Prince of Peace was correctly notified by the angelic anthem. But men by wicked hands took Him, imprisoned Him, and murdered Him, finding no fault in Him. A sense of the most common justice would tell us that "Peace on earth" must be postponed till the murder of the Just One be investigated and avenged, and He shall return in His glory to establish His kingdom in peace. So He taught us: "When ye shall hear of wars and commotions, be not terrified, for these things must first come to pass. And when these things begin to come to pass, *then look up, and lift up your head; for your redemption draweth nigh.*" "Our God shall come, and shall not keep silence." Men have to beat their "ploughshares into swords" (Joel iii. 10), before they beat their "swords into ploughshares" (Isa. ii. 4). Science can tell us much of human steps rising up to heaven; it can tell us nothing of that ladder let down from heaven to earth, on which angels ascend and descend. Nothing but "a sword" can be for the earth, till the Prince of Peace is accepted as Lord,—

> "When the crowns that are now
> Round the false one's brow,
> Shall be worn by earth's rightful Lord."

Not only have we the widest circle, "the highest," giving glory to God by the mission of Christ, and the more limited one, "earth," gaining peace, but we have the condition of the individuals on earth detailed.

3. "Good pleasure in men." For this we believe is by far the most correct and satisfactory explanation of the original. "Good will to men" is in every way unsatisfactory, weak, and untenable. The Douay, and several Protestant editions take

this as a part of the second clause, making it, "Peace on earth among men of God's good pleasure" (reading the genitive, and not the nominative); the Douay explaining it, that there is peace on earth among Roman Catholics (which there is not), and the Protestants, that there is peace on earth among God's elect (which there is not). We believe "God's good pleasure in men" solves all the difficulties. The universe, the earth and men, are thus thought of in three parts of this ' *Gloria.*" It is the same thought as "This is my Beloved Son, in whom I am *well pleased*" (see *eudokia*, in Matt. xi. 26; Luke x. 21; Rom. x. 1; Eph. i. 5-9; Phil. i. 15; ii. 13; 2 Thess. i. 2, besides the frequent use of the verb). God was now for the first time well pleased with a man; saw his good pleasure in a man, and the divinely-given guarantee that, not only in this man, but on the many men to be saved by, identified with, and sanctified through this man, His good pleasure should rest with complacency. His delight shall be in the sons of men; in individuals now, but in the whole earth as such, by and by, when men shall be blessed in Him, and call Him blessed; when none shall say to his neighbour, "Know the Lord, because all shall know Him," and universal peace shall be on the earth, and this little planet shall choir forth, without discord, among the other orbs of God, its true note of praise, blending with all others in "Glory to God in the highest."

"WHO DELIVERED US, AND DOTH DELIVER, AND WILL DELIVER."

2 Cor. i. 9, 10.

GOD'S works may be near us, around us, but His person unknowable. At Sinai we hear a holy God speaking to His creatures, and there we find a God of inflexible justice. In this text we listen to God, not as a mystery, nor a destroyer, but a deliverer. Here we find Him not as one whose work is to garnish the heavens, or deck the earth, but a God who has come Himself to deliver us. Man has tried to conquer death, but he is as far from it as ever. Money may go far and do much, but death is the end of all. Your fame may extend far, but death is the limit of fame. But the Apostle speaks here of more than the mere separation of soul and body, when he says "so great a death," namely, that of the separation of man from God. God's way is not to shirk the question of death, but to interpose as a deliverer from it.

When the Israelites were bitten by the fiery serpents, God did not remove them, but he comes and says, " Here is my way." The serpent of brass must be put on a pole, and *whosoever*, however severely bitten, looked on it, was healed. Some might have tried their own ways of deliverance, by attempting to kill the serpents near to them, by endeavoring to staunch their bleeding wounds, by using remedies of their own devising. But God's way is above and beyond all man's plans, and when man takes God at His word, then God is honored. All the bitten Israelites had the sentence of death in themselves, but if any would look right away from self, and take God's method, it mattered not how many, nor how virulent his bites might be, he was healed.   When the question of man's deliverance from eternal death comes in, we want nothing between the sinner and the Saviour.   Many want to come to God's ministers and get a certificate from them that they are saved; but the question is, Have you found yourself in God's Word?   God's Word comes as to a rational being, and the question is, "What does He say?"   A minister can only say to the anxious one, "There is the truth of God; that is what God says."   He cannot interfere between God and the sinner; his work is done when he has brought the sinner face to face with what God says.   The Apostle Paul took the sentence of death in himself; then he accepted God's way of deliverance.

We find deliverance here, in three aspects,—

1. Delivered.
2. Doth deliver.
3. Will deliver.

Deliverance in the past, leading up to the present, and going on continuously into the future.   We get deliverance in the past, as justification, in the present, as sanctification and cleansing.   There is great misconception oftentimes concerning the cleansing blood.   It is not only true that it *has cleansed*, but it *is cleansing;* once applied it is of continual efficacy. The holiest saint needs the blood continually, at every moment.

Take the life-boat as a picture of this deliverance, for it is not help that the shipwrecked mariner needs, but deliverance. Therefore the life-boat carries no luggage, no boards, or anything wherewith to patch up the wreck; but the shipwrecked ones must leave all, and simply drop into the life-boat.   Some try to save people by making them religious.   This will never do.   Self must be left.   A man is willing, it may be, to leave his sins, but not his good deeds; but all must be relinquished. In the life-boat we are delivered from the great wreck, but not yet ashore.   There is a present as well as a past deliverance needed, and the same who delivered us from so great a death, is delivering still between the wreck and the shore; and as we look at the lights in the harbor, we say, "In whom we trust that He will yet deliver us."

The important point is the first step.   Faith consists in letting go, as well as laying hold.   As the life-boat comes under the wreck, and the crew drop into it, so must we let go of al other hope, and cling only to Christ. Let us not trust in our faith, nor repentance, nor conversion; the devil may argue us out of these, as he argued Adam and Eve out of Paradise. Put yourself into the middle of a text, as, "All we like sheep have gone astray. We have turned every one to his own way." Is that true of you? Well, then, having walked in at one end of it, walk out at the other: "And the Lord hath laid on Him the iniquity of us all." Resist the devil with a text. He can soon make out that you are not a believer; but get in at the sinner door. He will never prove you are not a sinner, and "Christ Jesus came into the world to save sinners."

Anchor to a text that is something worth gripping. Many look to their feelings, to something within, to see if they are saved. What would you think of a man who should drop the anchor into the hold of a ship, and say, "We must keep it on board; we must not lose sight of it." Let go; cast the anchor outside; then fixed on rock outside, the anchor is fulfilling its function. Faith goes outward, not inward; Christward, not selfward; has to do with the Word of God, not feelings.

"HE CAME WHERE HE WAS."

Luke x. 30-35.

"BY CHANCE a certain priest *came that way.*" "And a Levite, when he was *at the place,* came and *looked.*" "But a certain Samaritan, as he journeyed, CAME WHERE HE WAS." So the Lord Jesus Christ did not stand away up in heaven, and say, "Come to Me;" He did not come half way; He did not come and say, "I will give you help." No. There are some people who speak about stepping-stones to the gospel. What an absurdity, when Christ has done all the work ! Where stands the cross? Between two malefactors. Did they need stepping-stones? Stepping-stones, indeed, to Him who says, "Him that cometh unto me, I will in no wise cast out !" There is only one illustration of stepping-stones spoken of in the Bible, and that was the altar of burnt-offering. The Bible itself says, "There shall be no steps to my altar." God would not allow a step to be put up : the altar had to be set on the sand within the reach of the lowest sinner. You do not need a pair of religious steps to help Christ to do His work.

I. "HE CAME WHERE HE WAS."

That is the gospel of God. He became one of us, that He might become one with us under our sin, that we might be saved, and become one with Him. The blessed Christ of God came to where we were. That is the most beautiful word to my soul, in all the tenth chapter of Luke. He came not to the palace, or to the house, but to the side of the devil-forsaken ditch. Remember, the devil had left—the thieves had left : they had nothing more to get out of the poor Jew. And so with the poor drunkard : when the landlord has taken his last penny and left him, Christ was waiting to be his friend. He "*came where he was.*" Beautiful sentence! I have seen a poor drunkard going to the public-house where he had spent his last penny, asking bread, and met by the landlord, who had got his money, with, "Go away or I will get a policeman to you." He has been stripped by the thieves. The Samaritan comes right down to the ditch where the Jew had been left, but does not say, you are too bad company for me. Yes, to those that the devil had cast out, He came to where they were. "Thank God," say some, "that I am not like other men!" But there is no distinction with God. You are not a whit better than the worst drunkard in creation. God has weighed you all in the scales, and He says there is not a bit of difference between you. In God's sight there is no difference. We would like to think there are degrees of guilt and of forgiveness; but God says there is not a bit of difference. Certainly, there are what men call greater sinners, and lesser sinners. Just like a man, for instance, wanting to get into the Life Guards. You may think yourself the biggest man in the village. The recruiting-sergeant does not care whether you are the biggest or smallest. He puts up his six foot measure. The man five feet six inches in height has no chance. And in a man five feet eleven and a half inches, there is, of course, a difference as to size; but in his case it is just the same as regards his exclusion from the Life Guards. So God says there is no difference between any of those who have sinned, and come short of the glory of God. It is not that you are a big sinner, or a little sinner; but you have come short. You may be five feet six inches, or five feet eleven and a half inches, or even more: it does not matter. This is the way we are leveled down. Take the opinion that God has of you. He puts you on a level with every sinner.

2. "HAD COMPASSION ON HIM."

"*He came where he was, and when he saw him, he had compassion on him, and went to him, and bound up his wounds, pouring in oil and wine.*" He did not leave him. It was not the theology of Christ to take him up to-day, and leave him to-morrow. He takes care of him, sets him on his own beast, takes him to an inn, and provides for him there. It is Christ's salvation. Christ has sent His Spirit to lead us through the journey, to support, to strengthen and guide us all the way through. He brought us to an inn. He takes His people to this pastor, or teacher, and He says to them, "There is a soul I have got saved. Keep him, house him, feed him well, and there is enough for you to keep a-going just now; and if you spend any more, when I come back I will repay you." I do not believe in these quarrelings and wranglings about churches, which are now so common, instead of looking to the poor wounded Jew lying beside them.

3. ALL DONE—ALL PAID.

What did the poor relieved Jew do now? He would ask, "What have I to pay?" "Oh! it is all for nothing. The Samaritan paid it all." We could suppose the man sitting looking out at the window, turned from his enmity to the Samaritans, waiting to thank his deliverer—as it says in Thessalonians, "turned to God from idols to serve the living and true God, and to wait for His Son from heaven." So the Jew was waiting for the Samaritan. Why is it we hear so little of the return of the good Samaritan? It would be awkward for many people if He did return just now. The next time Christ comes He will not be despised and rejected. "Behold, He cometh with clouds; and every eye shall see Him, and they also which pierced Him: and all kindreds of the earth shall wail because of Him." The unfaithful servant said, "My Lord delayeth His coming," and began to smite his fellow-servants, and to eat and drink with the drunken. But "the Lord of that servant shall come in a day when he looketh not for him, and in an hour that he is not aware." The man that is not quite square with his books, does not like his master to come in unawares upon him, and look at them. But there are even genuine Christians, and behold they all slumber and sleep. Does not Satan manage it well? "But He that shall come will come, and will not tarry." And when I come, He says, "I will repay thee for what thou didst unto Me."

THE WHOLE ARMOUR.

EPH. vi. 11-18.

THE Master says it is our weakness He requires in order to show His strength. I bring you St. Paul's words: "Finally, my brethren, be strong in the Lord, put on the whole armour of God." Let me remind you that we have a great Trinity in our favour—Father Son, and Holy Ghost— the Father loving us from all eternity, the Son sending us the Holy Spirit, the Holy Spirit keeping us, by throwing us back on Christ, who again throws us back on the Father. "Holy Father, keep through Thine own name those whom thou hast given me." But we have a trinity against us—the world, the flesh, the devil. Satan aims primarily, not at us, but through us at the Prince of Peace. The power to meet the flesh is the spirit, the power to meet the world is the Father, the power to overcome the devil is Christ. It is our intrinsic *red-hotness* that must make us intolerable to the world. There is still war in the world, there will be war to the end. The Christian's attitude is war—righteousness against sin. "Put on the whole armour of God;" mark, this is not to cover us in the sight of God. God has put on us Christians, His righteousness; it is not the *robe*, but the *armour* we are bidden to put on. Soldiers, not invalids, strong men, not babes, are wanted to fight the battles of the Lord.

"Loins girt about with truth," not truth in the Word, but subjective truth; a man must be true to himself; God must have a true witness; falseness of any kind entangles him. This Epistle, which gives us the highest thoughts about our standing, comes down to the plain truth, such as "speak truth."

Then comes the "breastplate of righteousness," not the righteousness which fits me for Heaven, but righteousness between man and man. The apostle's injunction is, "Owe no man anything but love." Then you can face the devil. How can you face him if you have done injustice to your fellow-man? "Feet shod with the preparation of the Gospel of peace." I have nothing to bear to the world but the Gospel of peace. If peace is the Gospel from me, the world are to know only my footfall as I bring the Gospel of peace. Next, the "shield of faith." This is the faith that shields me, not the faith that saves me. "Helmet of salvation." If a man goes without the assurance of salvation, he goes into battle with his head uncovered, exposed to danger at every blow. As an old divine says, salvation is a helmet, not a nightcap; for battle, not for idleness. "Sword of the Spirit." No weapon formed on earth is like the word of God; we believe in its temper and its steel. In modern warfare, shield and breastplate are not used, but the sword has to take their place; so more and more we have to use the Word of God for every purpose of defence and attack. I was puzzled for a time with the inveteracy with which Deuteronomy has been attacked, till I remembered that it was the armoury from which our Lord drew His weapons with which to foil the tempter. No marvel Satan hates the remembrance of his defeat, and the texts that quelled him. We might also find in these texts a motto for each day of our life. The source of strength—"Man shall not live by bread alone, but by every word of God." The danger of losing it—"Thou shalt not tempt the Lord thy God." The power for maintaining it—"Thou shalt worship the Lord thy God, and Him only shalt thou serve." "Stand fast in the Lord." You may have the finest sword and yet lack power to wield it. What will nerve your arm? "Praying always with all prayer and supplication in the Spirit." All prayer, is all power—no prayer, is no power. God give us to put on all this armour!

WITNESSING FOR GOD.

Acts i. 8.

IN our peculiar work, as preachers, we must be REAL, if others are to be benefited by our ministry. And if we desire that others shall be sealed through our labours, we must be sealed ourselves. No man can expect a blessing, unless he goes into the work with the power of the Holy Ghost. The Holy Ghost is essential to the dispensation of the gospel. Believers sometimes make a mistake with regard to the Holy Spirit, especially in reference to His office in the salvation of sinners. There is a door which God has opened into the holy of holies, and there is no other way to get near God but by that door. Jesus is the door—the only door—by which we can enter; but it is in vain to expect that men will receive the Son, and enter by the door, until they have been inclined to receive Him, and have been drawn by the Holy Spirit.

It is in vain to expect that men will be saved, or even led to seek salvation, by listening to elaborate and beautiful discourses upon the wondrous work of creation, or the beauties of God in His providence.

You can never lead a man to God, by simply telling him about God. It is a hard truth, but it is, however, a correct one. "No man cometh unto the Father, but by me." Again, "No man can come to Me, except the Father, who hath sent Me, draw him." These two truths cover the whole circle. You cannot bring any man to God save by the Spirit, and you cannot have the Spirit without Jesus. Through the Spirit we can approach the Infinite, by Him who hath condescended to make himself finite for us. We are to rejoice in the Holy Ghost, of whom I have been speaking, as the instrument of our salvation. If we would see fruit, we should teach Him, preach Him. He is ever present with His people. Let us seek that His pervading and energizing spirit should be operating upon our hearts; and that He will take of the things of Christ, and reveal them plainly unto us.

You, my brethren, are the instruments raised by God to do His work in an important part of the vineyard. Oh, let us pray that we ourselves may know the truth, and be filled with the Spirit—the earnest of our inheritance.

THE Shepherd seeks the lost sheep "UNTIL he finds it" (Luke xv. 4). And it is only the lost sheep that lies in the pathway of the seeking Shepherd. If I take the place of a lost sinner, and nothing else, it is not so much my part to seek Christ, as His to seek me. This is grace. He seeks *until* He finds; He does not stop in His search *until* He and we meet. Alas! our part is only straying.

The word of LAW would be: "They that seek Me early shall find Me" (Prov. viii. 17). And the consequence of man being put on this ground is stated by God Himself: "*There is none that seeketh after God.*" (Rom. iii. 2.)

The holy, just and good law of God came demanding of us love to God, and proved that what God justly demands from man He does not get, and cannot get; so that without exception, it may be said of all men who ought to have sought after God, "*There is none that seeketh after God.*"

GRACE comes in now, and says, "I will seek you, and I will seek *until* I find." Thank God, it is He who breaks in upon us, and not we upon Him. We would willingly remain among those who "forget" God. Our wills are free only to wander, and get farther from Him. In fact, the first thing God does in breaking in upon our enmity is, "to make us willing."

Our part is to take the place of a sinner and nothing else. Most people believe they are sinners, but comparatively few believe that they are sinners and nothing else but *sinners.*

As truly as He hath shown us that we are lost, and nothing but lost, so surely can we gladly claim that seeking Shepherd; for He seeks *until* He finds.

Nothing stops Him in His search—not all the hatred of man

or devils ; not all the malice and spite and envy of the chief priests ; not all the murmurings of the Pharisees and scribes ; not all the waywardness of the wandering sheep ; nor the indifference and degradation of those for whom He is searching. He will have His joy—that joy that rejoices not, UNTIL it finds.

2. But there is another and awful " UNTIL " in Luke xvii. 27 : " They did eat, they drank, they married wives, they were given in marriage, UNTIL the day that Noah entered into the ark, and the flood came and destroyed them all ; and as it was in the days of Noah, so shall it be also in the days of the Son of Man."

That little word " UNTIL " tells out the sad story of what man is. Men will please themselves, let God's claims or God's grace be where they may. And thus will they go on "UNTIL."

But every history has its UNTIL. The course of the vilest infidel is brought to a close by an UNTIL. The world's race to destruction will be consummated in that UNTIL. Vain are the thoughts of those who think of the gradual conversion of the world. They go on as JESUS CHRIST said they would—careless, and wholly engrossed with their own affairs, *until* the Lord comes.

This is not each man knowing the Lord "from the least to the greatest." The world goes on in rebellion and self-pleasing *until* the Lord comes and sweeps them away, as with the besom of destruction. May we now be as men that believe this, and tell out the virtues of a Christ for sinners, *until* that day.

Few of us, I fear, realize that there is a way of *keeping* out of hell, but no way of *getting* out of it.

That blasphemous infidelity, that the punishment of the wicked will not be eternal, is sapping the very foundation of Christian action. What is the use of Christian effort ? Let us take things quietly, if, after suffering for awhile in a purgatorial hell, all are to be restored !

May God have mercy on us for our lukewarmness, and stir us all up to believe His simple Word, that *until* Jesus comes men will go on in their mad career, but that this is the limit to their proud waves ; for we again read, that—

The heavens will receive Jesus Christ "UNTIL the times of restitution of all things, which God hath spoken," etc. And this *until*, while being glorious, and final salvation to the Christ-receiver, restoration to God's ancient people, and emancipation

to a groaning creation, is the time of destruction of all Christ's
rejectors.   For God says (Acts iii. 21, 22), that in the time of
the restitution of all things, " it shall come to pass, that *every*
soul which will not hear that Prophet (JESUS) shall be DESTROYED
from among the people."

" Let God be true, and every man a liar."   Christ will remain
away UNTIL this time of mingled salvation and destruction.—
salvation to all who were sought and found by Him ; *destruction*
to all who rejected Him, it being one of God's impossibilities
to renew such to repentance.   Solemn words !   May we make
our calling and election sure !

"He came not to call the righteous, but *sinners*."   Thus
called and thus saved, we can patiently wait, leaning on the
precious Word, while even some that profess Christ's name are
leaning to their own understandings, and taking their own ideas
as their light ; or while a godless, reckless world is posting on
to destruction, taking no warning, dancing madly, blindly on,
UNTIL (and what an *until* it will be !)—*until* He shall gird His
sword on His thigh, to slay and not to heal ; and, in the midst
of their calamity and dreadful fear, His word is, " *I will laugh
at your calamity ; I will mock when your fear cometh.*"

THE
BRITISH EVANGELIST.

MONTHLY ONE PENNY.

EDITED BY THE

WIDOW OF DR. W. P. MACKAY,

HULL.

Contents for the coming year:—

Expositions of John's Gospel, by the late Dr. Mackay.

Leading thoughts on the International Sunday School Lessons, for the help of Teachers.

Gospel articles by the Rev. Dr. Fraser, London, and others.

Send address and One dollar

TO

MRS. MACKAY,

SO. MORNINGSIDE DRIVE,

EDINBURGH.

AND FOUR COPIES WILL BE POSTED MONTHLY

Few Books of a Religious Character have been accorded such Hearty and Universal Endorsement from all Denominations.

The Christian's Secret of a Happy Life

By H. W. S.

THIRTY-THIRD THOUSAND.

With introduction by Rev. H. M. Parsons and Rev. John Potts, D.D. Cloth, Gilt extra, 75c ; Cloth Plain, 50c.; Paper 30c. *For Distribution.* Paper Cover, at $2.50 per doz. post-paid.

Baptist Commendation.

"We are delighted with this book It reaches to the very core of Christian experience, and is eminently experimental in its teachings. It meets the doubts and difficulties of conscientious seekers after the bread and water of life, but whose efforts result only in alternate failure and victory. The author, without claiming to be a theologian, sends out the results of a happy and rich experience to help others into a happy Christian life."—*Baptist Weekly.*

Presbyterian Endorsement.

"The book is so truly and reverentially devout in its spirit that it disarms criticism. It contains so much that is sound and practical, so much that, if heeded, will make our lives better, happier and more useful, that the intelligent reader who really wishes to lead a life 'hid with Christ in God,' can scarcely fail to derive profit from its perusal." —*Interior.*

Methodist Word of Praise.

"We have not for years read a book with more delight and profit, It is not a theological book. No effort is made to change the theological views of anyone. The author has a rich experience, and tells it in a plain and delightful manner."—*Christian Advocate.*

United Brethren's Approval.

"We have seldom met with a more interesting volume, abounding throughout with apt illustrations ; we have failed to find a dry line from title page to finis."—*Religious Telescope.*

Congregational Comment.

"It contains much clear, pungent reasoning and interesting incident. It is a practical and experimental lesson taught out of God's word, and is worthy of *universal* circulation."—*Church Union.*

S. R. BRIGGS, Toronto Willard Tract Depository, Toronto, Canada.